Loughboro Inl.
Bute Inl.
Homatheo
L.Ande
Port
Lilloet R.
Toba Inl.
Squamish
Redonda
Desolation S.
Uahdose
La Lia R.
manor Str.
Sarah
C.Mudge
Savary I.
Scotch Fir Pt.
Jervis Inl.
Clowhom
Texada
Gulf
Howe Sd.
A N D
of
Lasquiti I.
Burrard Inl.
Hornel
G
Central L.
Nanaimo
Cameron I.
orgia
New
Westmr
Nitinat
Alberni C.
Pt.
Roberts
lay Sd.
Semiamo R.
C.Beale
Cowichen R.
Nitinat
P.S. Juan
Saanich B.

THE
CAPTIVE OF NOOTKA

CAPTIVE OF NOOTKA.

ADVENTURES OF JOHN R. JEWETT.

PHILADELPHIA:

LIPPINCOTT, GRAMBO & CO.

1854.

THE
CAPTIVE OF NOOTKA
OR THE

Adventures
of
John R. Jewitt

YE GALLEON PRESS
FAIRFIELD, WASHINGTON

1996

Library of Congress Cataloging-in-Publication Data

The captive of Nooka, or, The adventures of John R. Jewitt. p.
cm.
Includes bibliographical references.
ISBN 0-87770-578-X (hard case). -- ISBN 0-87770-579-8
(paper)
1. Jewitt, John Rodgers, 1783-1821. 2. Nootka Indians. 3.
Indian captivities--British Columbia.
E99.N85J472 1996
971.1'2004979--dc20

96-4600
CIP

MACUINA

This is a likeness of the Nootkan chief, Maquina, as taken from a Spanish book, the Relacion del viage hecho por las goletas Sutil y Mexicana en el ano de 1792 para reconocer el estrecho de Fuca, *Madrid, 1802. The original drawing was presumably made in the year 1792.*

PARTING OF JEWETT AND MAQUINA.

CONTENTS.

CHAPTER I.

CHAPTER II.

CHAPTER III.

CHAPTER IV.

CHAPTER V.

CHAPTER VI.

CHAPTER VII.

CHAPTER VIII.

CHAPTER IX.

CHAPTER X.

CHAPTER XI.

CHAPTER XII.

CHAPTER XIII.

CHAPTER XIV.

CHAPTER XV.

CHAPTER XVI.

CHAPTER XVII.

CHAPTER XVIII.

CHAPTER XIX.

CHAPTER XX.

CHAPTER XXI.

CHAPTER XXII.

CHAPTER XXIII.

CHAPTER XXIV.

John R. Jewitt.
From a pen-and-ink portrait furnished by his great-grandson,
Frank R. Jewitt, of Cleveland Heights, Ohio.

CAPTIVE OF NOOTKA.

CHAPTER I.

Nativity of Jewitt—his father's views—John goes to school—his master—his studies—he gives up Latin—is taken from school—is intended for a surgeon—does not like the profession—concludes to be a blacksmith—his father removes to Hull—he shows a taste for the sea—resolves to be a sailor.

JOHN R. JEWITT was born in Boston, England, on the 21st of May, 1783. His father was an industrious and respectable blacksmith, who, while he was shaping and moulding the iron on the anvil, did not forget that he had the minds of his children to shape and prepare for still more important purposes.

He knew that the iron, when it had fulfilled the end for which he was fitting it, must rust and crumble away. But he felt that the immortal minds of his offspring, however, they might be suffered to rust here, must carry the effects of neglect into eternity.

His wife died when his children were very young, and the important part of bending the twig in a right direction, so as to make it grow to a goodly tree, devolved on his parental care, alone.

As a good and wise father, he sought to make early moral and religious impressions, while the minds of his little charge were young and tender; and knowing that theory, to be of any use, must be wedded to practice, he made his own example an illustration of his teaching.

With his truly blacksmith motto, ' strike while the iron is hot,' he felt that the most important bent of the never-dying soul, for its happiness here, as well as hereafter, must be made in an early state, while it was soft and warm, and that, in doing this, there was no time to be lost.

His eldest son he intended for his own profession; but our hero, John, not being of so robust a constitution as his brother, to enable him to stand before the furnace, and wield the hammer, was destined to the less laborious, though not less trying and painful office of a surgeon.

John was, therefore, at the age of twelve years, sent from home, for the advantage of better schooling than could be obtained in his native town, and placed under the care of a Mr. Moses, at Donnington, about twenty miles from his own place of residence.

Whether Mr. Moses was, or was not, a lineal descendant of the Jewish lawgiver, whose name he bore, I am not able to say.

But he was a very good lawgiver in his own dominions, and preserved excellent order in the academy over which he was set as head, to 'teach the young idea how to shoot.'

He taught John R. Jewitt's ideas to shoot into arithmetic, surveying, navigation, English grammar, &c.; but into *Latin*, John did not much like to have his master direct them.

He had a natural impediment in his speech, that troubled and embarrassed him in scanning Latin; and concluding that his tongue was never made for the purpose, he gave it up, altogether, when he had obtained his father's consent to his so doing.

It is most probable, however, that John had in his mind, a greater impediment to learning the dead language, than any in his articulation. He did not love the Latin; but he could amuse his friends, whole evenings together, by singing to them, and this he often did, having a fine, pleasant voice, and a great taste for music.

Two years passed off very pleasantly with him, at Donnington; for he loved his master, Moses; and the master was attached to his pupil;—his father came often to see him—he had many friends, school-fellows, and relatives there; and, in short, he has since declared the two years he spent at this school, to be the happiest period of his life.

At length, the time arrived, when his father, thinking it proper for him to begin his apprentice-

ship, and the study of the profession he was to pur-
sue, took him from school, with the view of putting
him under the tuition of an eminent surgeon, from
whom, he had reason to believe, that his youngest
son would acquire as much skill at the lancet and
the probe, as his elder one would, from himself, at
the bellows and the forge.

But, as a proof of what I have just said about
early impressions and inclinations being the stron-
gest and most lasting, John's mind revolted at the
undertaking of a surgical profession, and his feelings all bore him, like a mighty current, towards
his father's anvil.

He had, from his infancy, been fond of going
into the shop and amusing himself, among the
workmen, by imitating, as far as he was able, their
motions; and he longed to accomplish such work
as he saw them do.

This taste and disposition now returned upon
him with such force, that he became unhappy at
the thought of not pursuing his father's business,

2   B

and he said so much, and evinced such an aversion to any other line of life, that he finally succeeded in gaining permission to go to the work of a blacksmith, in his father's shop.

But, it will hereafter appear, that, had he yielded implicitly to the first wish and design of his good parent, and brought his own will and inclination into subjection to his, who knew better than he did, what was best for him, he would have escaped the danger and sufferings, to which, making choice of a profession for himself, paved the way.

His father had now married again, and his step-mother was an excellent woman, which, added to the other charms of the paternal establishment, made his life very happy.

About a year after his removal from school, his father removed to Hull, which being one of the best ports in England, and a place of much trade, offered great advantages to one of his business.

At Hull, Mr. Jewitt had a great deal to do about the iron-work of the shipping, which not only led him often to the vessels, where John liked exceedly well to accompany him, but, also, brought many seamen to his shop and his house.

Among his customers at Hull, were many of the Americans, who frequented the port, and whose conversation and characters pleased Mr. Jewitt so much, that he often sought and cultivated an acquaintance with them, which his business alone would not have demanded.

John loved to listen to the stories of the sailors; and their merry-making accounts of the adventures they had met with, kindled in his young mind a strong desire to go to sea, and see the world too.

He read 'Cook's Voyages,' and many other voyages, till at last, he began to feel, that, to circumnavigate the globe, were a thing far easier for him, than to stay on it, and not do this; and his thoughts whirled round it, much faster than the earth whirls upon her axis; while he came, in his own mind, to the conclusion, that, it was for this very purpose, that his good master Moses had been turning his attention to the study of navigation.

He had, like many other boys, who get on tiptoe to see the world, a thousand gay dreams of other nations and other realms; and happy had it been for him, as it would be for them, had all ended in dreams.

But John R. Jewitt proved, as hundreds of others have done, that, sailing from port to port, by the help of a book, on one's pillow, or snugly lodged in the window recess, or the rocking-chair, is a very different affair, from climbing the shrouds in the tempest—or when the icicles jingle at his ears, from the frozen rigging.

Well, John had lived four years with his father, at Hull, when, in the summer of 1802, the American ship Boston, of Boston, Massachusetts, arrived.

Her owners, Messrs. F. & T. Amory, had destined her to take in, at Hull, a cargo of such goods as should be suitable for a trade with the Indians, on the North-west coast of America, to which place she was to proceed, to exchange her cargo for one of furs and skins; then she was to depart for China, for another traffic, and thence for home.

At Hull, the ship needed repairs of so extensive a kind, as to detain her long enough for Mr. Jewitt and his family to become well acquainted with Captain Salter, her commander, her officers, and men.

Captain Salter and the mates used to pass many evenings at Mr. Jewitt's house; and John, who never lacked ears, when such visitors were present, took it upon himself to do much to entertain them, and greatly won their favor.

Captain Salter asked him one day, in a jocose manner, if he would like to go to sea with him.

The question was, to our young hero's imagination, like the spark that falls from the flint into the tinder-box, and he began to think that the time had really come when he was to see the world. Captain Salter saw that John was serious, and he began to be serious himself, and spoke to Mr. Jewitt on the subject.

He really felt a deep interest in the young man, and told Mr. Jewitt what a fine opportunity it would be for his son, to make the voyage to China, and then to return with him to the United States, where he might do, probably, better for himself, than he could by remaining in England, &c. &c.; till it was finally agreed that John should ship as armorer, on board the Boston, and thus take his first voyage.

CHAPTER II.

*John ships as armorer—the ship's cargo—Mr. Jewitt's advice—
John sails—is seasick—gets well—goes to work—arrival and
stay at St. Catharine's—sails again for Cape Horn—passes
it—music—porpoises.*

JOHN was a very ingenious youth and he was
well skilled in his profession. He understood the
business he undertook as armorer, perfectly, and no
one could outdo him in giving polish and edge to
the steel blade, or make a smoother gun-barrel.

His locks snapped well; and he fancied that all
his plans would go off as readily and successfully
as his muskets. He thought the one now on foot,
was to hit the mark exactly; and that he had not
been so long aiming in vain, at seeing other parts
of the world.

It was agreed that he should have for his wages,
thirty dollars a month; and his father put into the

hands of Captain Salter, a certain sum of money, which, added to what should be due for his service, was to be laid out in furs, at the North-west coast, and these exchanged, when the ship should arrive at China, for such goods as would turn to profit when she returned to America.

Such was the plan laid for John to begin the world for himself. But, as many a tree will put forth fair leaves and blossoms, and yet yield no fruit, so it turned out with the promises of John's making his fortune at a jump.

You have all, my young readers, heard the anecdote of the poultry-girl, who, with her basket of eggs on her head, had her brain filled with the profit she should make on them, when they should become so many chickens; and anticipating the pleasure she should take in wearing the green gown, that was to be bought, when these chickens should be full grown and carried to market, gave her head a toss and her basket a fall.

You remember how all her hopes were then dashed with the contents of the broken egg-shells, on the pavement; which gives rise to the proverb of 'counting the chickens before they are hatched.'

Thus it proved with John. His hopes were soon crushed!

He set out, however, with fair prospects, with good advice, and in good company. Everything that could conduce to his convenience and comfort, was prepared by his excellent father; who had an iron forge erected for him, on the deck of the ship, and a vice-bench put in one corner of the steerage, so that, in bad weather, he might work below.

The ship's cargo consisted of English cloths, Dutch blankets, looking-glasses, beads, knives, razors, &c., with sugar, molasses, twenty hogsheads of rum, a great quantity of ammunition, pistols, cutlasses, and three thousand muskets and fowling-pieces.

All was now ready for sea; and when John had taken leave of all his other friends, his father went with him to the vessel, where, a moment before she sailed, he took him aside, and gave him, with deep emotion, the following excellent advice, which it

C

may be well for many a youth, not so old as John, to bear in mind, for he was now about nineteen.

'We now, my son, are going to part, and He only, to whom all things are known, knows if we are ever to meet again in this world. But, in whatever part of the world your lot may be cast, bear it ever in mind, that on your own conduct alone, depends your success in life and your peace in death.

'Be honest, industrious, frugal, and temperate. Let the Bible be your guide; and rely on its Author as your first and best friend. Then, whatever may befall you, you will have for your support in every trial, the consoling thought, that your dependence is on one who can bring good out of evil, and who never deserts those who put their trust in him.

'In short, my son, make it your determination to lead an honest and a Christian life; and remember that when your place is found empty at our table, it will not be so in our hearts; and that our first wish will be to hear from you.

'And now may the blessing of Him, who "holds

the winds in his fists," and the "ocean in the hollow of his hand," be upon you!'

It was on the 3d of September, 1802, that, in company with several other American vessels, bound to different ports, the Boston sailed from the Downs, with a serene, blue sky above, a peaceful sea below, and her white sails swelled with a fresh and favorable breeze.

As the vessel went on her watery way, and the billows gave her alternately a heave and a plunge, the head of our young hero, who had never been out of sight of the land before, began to turn and to swim, till he was fully convinced that the world must be as round as a bullet, but without the leaden propensity to lie still where it was placed.

He was visited with a sudden loss of appetite— his cheeks and his lips grew pale as the canvass about him; and his stomach sympathized in the motion of the waves. He was, for several of the first days, prostrated in the full enjoyment of the unenviable and unpitied condition, into which sea-sickness brings its subject.

SHIP BOSTON SAILS FROM THE DOWNS.

But in a few days, John recovered from this malady—his appetite returned—his color returned—his head became steady, and he stood up on his feet again, like a man.

As he did this, he looked behind, but saw nothing of the shores of old England; he looked before, but the sky and the sea were all that met his eye; so he turned for occupation to his forge.

With good health and spirits, he went to work, and employed himself in fair weather, making knives, daggers, and small hatchets for the Indian trade. When it stormed, he went below, and busied himself in filing and polishing them.

He liked, however, to lend a hand now and then, when the men were managing the rigging, so as to get a little initiated into the business of a sailor. And he loved, when his day's work was done, to look round on the mighty scene of the heavens and the deep, till his mind was lost in contemplating the greatness and the power of their Creator and Sustainer.

John found great comfort in reflecting that,

though he was far from the house of his earthly parent, the home of his heavenly Father was everywhere; and that his eye would keep watch through the darkest night, and his hand be at the helm, amid the most threatening seas.

A pleasant sail of twenty-nine days brought the ship to the Island of St. Catharine, on the coast of Brazil, where Captain Salter intended to stop, to replenish his stock of wood and water, and obtain fresh provisions.

The island belonged to the Portuguese, and on entering the port, the ship was saluted by guns from the fort, which compliment she returned, and passed in.

The next day, she was honored with a visit from his excellency, the governor of the island, and his suite, and her crew treated by them with much respect and politeness.

At this island, the Boston remained four days; and the men found it a very good stopping-place, for a purpose like theirs, as it abounds with springs of sweet, clear water, and with fine oranges, plantains, bananas, &c.

They took in such supplies as to render it unnecessary for them to stop at any of the Sandwich Islands, and put to sea.

On the twenty-fifth of December, they passed Cape Horn, which they had made thirty-six days before, but had been repeatedly driven back by adverse winds; the weather being extremely tempestuous while they were doubling, or passing round the cape.

When they had gained this point, all seemed smooth again. The weather was fine; and taking advantage of the monsoon, or trade-wind, they went on with the greatest ease, having, for the space of a fortnight, hardly to make a tack, or reef a top-sail.

Captain Salter was an old experienced India ship-master, who knew how to keep good order among his men, without their being constantly at work; and when their situation did not require this, he loved to see them enjoy themselves, as they now had an opportunity of doing, till John began to think a sailor's life was a pretty easy and merry one.

There was a fine musical band on board, and during the serene, pleasant evenings they had while making their way on the Southern ocean, Captain Salter used to order them to play for the entertainment of the crew.

This was a treat he was very fond of giving them on Saturday nights, as a sort of a welcome to the coming Sabbath.

Music at such an hour, and in such a scene, must have sounded delightfully, while the waters gurgled round the prow of the ship, and the ocean's hoarse voice sang bass, in the distance.

Now and then a whale or a flying-fish would let itself be seen above the surface of the water; but whether it was to listen to the music, or not, it has not yet been ascertained—the reader will be able to judge of the probability of this.

They saw, also, frequent shoals of porpoises,

coming towards the ship; the purpose or business of which, I believe was not then, nor ever has been clearly understood; but of their appearance I will speak in the next chapter.

CHAPTER III.

Description of a shoal of porpoises—albatrosses seen—arrival at Nootka Sound—the natives came on board—the Indian king described—intercourse with the savages— their visits—Maquana breaks the gun—Captain Salter offends him—his dignified deportment when angry.

A SHOAL of porpoises was to John R. Jewitt a very novel and interesting sight. They looked at a distance like a multitude of small black waves, rolling one over the other, in great confusion and very quick motion.

As they came gamboling along towards the vessel in this way, all on board was in a bustle. Every hand was busy to get the harpoons ready to strike; and those who were the most skilful, took the most favorable stands, to make the deadly thrust, as the unsuspecting porpoises sported beside the ship.

The porpoise, or sea-hog, when struck and drawn

on board by the harpoon, utters most piteous cries, resembling those of an infant, till it dies. It was very shocking to John, to hear these sounds of distress, when the first victim was taken.

The sailors afterwards told him that, if one of these animals received a wound, without being taken, all the others in the troop, attracted by his blood, would leave the vessel and chase him till they should overtake him, and then tear him to pieces and devour him.

Our young mariner found the flesh of the porpoise a very palatable dish, after being so long as he had been, without any thing fresh; and when cut into steaks and broiled, he thought its taste resembled that of beef done in the same way.

He saw on his passage, a great number of albatrosses, one of which Captain Salter shot, and measuring his extended wings, from one extremity to the other, found that they measured fifteen feet. The albatross is a large bird of the goose tribe, whose feathers are brown and white.

Pursuing a northward course, after passing Cape

Horn, the ship arrived, on the 12th of March, 1803, at Woody Point, in Nootka Sound, on the Northwest coast of America.

Captain Salter made up the sound towards Nootka, a few miles north of the Indian town, on the land bordering the sound, in order to get supplies of wood and water, before he proceeded up the coast for trade.

He wished to avoid being seen, so as to escape molestation from the Indians of the village, which was situated on Friendly Cove.

When some of the men, who took the boat and went out to sound for a good anchoring place, returned, they said they had found one, near a small island, which was well protected from the sea, and had plenty of wood and water; and which lay about half a mile from the coast.

Accordingly, the ship drew up to this place, and was anchored; though not without being observed by the natives.

The next morning an Indian canoe was seen from the ship, gliding along towards it, manned

ARRIVAL OF THE SHIP AT NOOTKA SOUND.

with a number of savages, who paddled their way up to the Boston, and came on board.

It was the king of the place, with his savage retinue; and an odd king, indeed, did he seem to John R. Jewitt, who knew what splendor and pomp surrounded his own king in England.

The name of the monarch of Nootka was *Maquina;* whose Indian majesty, as he stood up in all his dignity, on the deck of the ship, might thus be described:

His person, about six feet in height, was straight and well formed; his face of the copper complexion, with good features and expression, but marked with what is not common among these people, a fine Roman nose. But his face, arms, and legs were, on this occasion, so disguised by paint, as almost to prevent their natural color from being seen.

Over each eyebrow was drawn a heavy black line, like a crescent, and his hair, long and black, was drawn up and tied in a bunch on the top of his head. It was oiled so as to shine, and then, strewed over with a fine white down, which gave it the appearance of being half covered with snow flakes.

His dress was a cloak of black sea-otter skin, which reached to his knees; and was fastened about the waist with a girdle of the cloth of the country, painted with various colors, and in a diversity of figures.

This cloth is made of the bark of a tree, and somewhat resembles straw-matting.

Maquina's attendants had their dresses made of it. The cloak, or mantle which they wore, was a square of this material, large enough to reach to the knee, and with places cut in the top for the arms to pass through.

The belt, being a strip of the same cloth, was about four inches wide, and whimsically figured.

Maquina had frequently visited the American and English vessels that came for trade on the coast; and if they did not take his furs, or if he had none to offer, the masters always treated him well, and generally gave him some little presents, which proved a sufficient inducement for him to visit the next vessel that came.

In this way he had learnt to understand a great many English words and expressions; and as it afterwards proved, he knew much more than Captain Salter dreamed of, till he found it out at the cost of his life.

He took the copper-colored monarch into his cabin, gave him a glass of drink, and fed him with biscuit and molasses, a treat that pleased him highly.

Both the king and his people seemed much gratified with the manner and the hospitality of the ship's crew; and after leaving them the first day, they returned the next, bringing with them more of the natives, and a good supply of fine fresh salmon, for which they took some trifling articles by way of pay.

It was not the intention of Captain Salter to make his purchases at this place, as there were not many furs to be obtained; but he wanted to get his stock of wood and water, so as not to be obliged to expose his men for these necessaries when they should be farther north, and among, what he considered, more barbarous tribes than the savages of Nootka.

While the hands were employed in laying in these provisions, John, the armorer, busied himself in repairing muskets, making tomahawks, knives, &c. and in doing such iron work as was needed on the ship.

Meantime, Maquina and his people kept up their visits, while Captain Salter, in order to prove that they had no hostile purposes, insisted that each should throw off his dress before he came on board, to satisfy him by showing that they had no arms concealed.

On the fifteenth, Maquina, attended by several of his chiefs, came on board. He was arrayed in his royal attire of otter-skin, and had his head newly powdered with white down; his face was painted with more than ordinary care, and almost covered with the ingredients he had used in beautifying it.

His chiefs were clad in the cloth of their country, of its original color, which is pale yellow. Their girdles were similar to that of the king, only not so wide.

Around the bottoms of their cloaks were painted borders, representing, in various colors, the heads of men and beasts, birds, and fishes.

The dress of the common people was like that of the chiefs, only the cloth was coarser, and they were not allowed to paint with more than one color, this being red.

Captain Salter invited them to dine with him, and his invitation was accepted. It was a great source of amusement to John, to see his copper-colored eminence, the king, and all the savage nobles, seat themselves and eat their dinner.

Their manner of sitting was similar to that of the Chinese. They crossed their legs and sat upon them; while they made their meal on ship-bread dipped in molasses, which was the only thing they would eat. They manifested a great aversion to every thing that tasted in the least of salt.

They appeared to enjoy their entertainment, and retired very pleasantly; the few following days, they kept up their trade; bringing the fresh salmon, and seemed satisfied with what they received in return for what was a great luxury to the seamen after living on salt provisions, as they had done, for some time.

About the nineteenth of the month, Maquina came on board the ship, and dined again. He talked a great deal with Captain Salter, and told him there were a great many wild ducks and geese near Friendly Cove.

Captain Salter gave him, upon this information, a fine double-barreled fowling-piece, with which he seemed greatly delighted, and went away.

The next day he came again on board, bringing with him nine pair of wild ducks, as a present to the Captain.

He also brought his new gun that he had received the day before, with one of the locks broken, which he showed to Captain Salter, telling him it was *peshak*, (bad.)

Captain Salter at this remark, which he thought a token of his gift being undervalued, and feeling irritated at seeing it so ill used too, showed signs of anger, and not knowing the extent of Maquina's understanding of the English, called him a liar, and told John to see how that fellow had ruined the beautiful fowling-piece. 'See,' said he, 'if you can mend it.'

The scene that now appeared on the deck, when described, speaks a loud moral. Captain Salter was in anger, and showed it, little dreaming of the bitter consequences that were to follow.

Maquina had understood him, and was in anger too; but he was silent and dignified—his emotions only appeared in the flashes of his keen black eye, and by his hand being rubbed hard upon his throat, and pressed on his bosom.

This, he afterwards told John, was to keep down his heart, that kept rising up in his throat, and nearly choked him.

The offended Indian monarch uttered not a word, but soon retired with his men, with a haughty air; and probably feeling his breast burning with stifled rage, and that unquenchable fire of revenge, which in the bosom of a savage is one of its most dearly loved principles, and never goes out but with his vital spark.

CHAPTER IV.

The natives induce some of the seamen to go on shore—they massacre the crew—John's life spared—the ship is run into the cove, and stranded—the savages welcome their king's return to the village.

On the twenty-second, many of the natives came out in the morning, as usual, to the ship, with their salmon, where they were joined, a few hours after, by Maquina, with many of his chiefs and others.

The king seemed in uncommonly good humor. He had over his face a hideous wooden mask, representing the head of some wild beast. In his hand he held a whistle, which he blew to a kind of tune to regulate the motions of his people, as they jumped, sang, and capered about on the deck, to the great amusement of the crew.

Maquina asked Captain Salter when he was going to sail. 'To-morrow,' was the reply.

'You love salmon—plenty in Friendly Cove—why not go catch some?' said he. The idea of having some caught to carry away, struck Captain Salter very pleasantly, and he concluded, after dinner, to send out some men to fish.

The steward was already on shore, at the watering-place, washing the Captain's clothes, when nine men, with the mate at their head, took the boats and the seine, and went in quest of salmon.

The king and his men had remained on board; and John had gone to work, cleaning muskets, at his vice-bench, in the steerage. When he had been below about an hour, he heard the seamen hoisting in the long boat.

In a few minutes after, he heard the sound of scuffling and great confusion on deck; and attempting to go up to see what was doing, he was seized, just as his head rose above board, by the hair, which one of the natives caught hold of; but the ribbon with which it was tied, slipping off in the hand of the Indian, let him fall back into the steerage.

Before he fell, however, he received a blow on the forehead by an axe in the hand of another savage, which left a deep wound; and he had time to see that the whole deck was one appalling scene of human slaughter.

The blow and the fall stunned him; and he probably lay some length of time senseless, for when he came to himself, he was covered with his own blood, and weak from its loss.

He felt as if arousing from some hideous dream —the hatch had been closed, and he was in darkness and gore—while the horrid yells and shouts of triumph sent from the savages over his head, convinced him that they had possession of the ship, and that they had done a great work of death, while not a single voice of one of the seamen was heard amid the wild sounds of barbarous exultation.

When the noise of singing, shouting, and yelling had a little subsided, Maquina ordered the hatch to be opened, and called, ' John, come up.'

John attempted to obey, but found himself almost

unable to move, and the eye over which the gash had been cut, was so swollen as to be nearly closed; while the other was half blinded by the blood that had flowed and fastened upon it.

Maquina seeing his condition, ordered his people not to injure him, but told them to help him up and wash and dress his wound, saying, that he knew how to make and mend their guns, and would be of great use to them, if preserved alive and unhurt.

This, John afterwards found, had been the cause of Maquina's ordering the hatch to be closed, during the dreadful scene that had taken place, so that he might not be numbered among the victims to the revenge of the Indians, as he intended his life should turn to their account, by keeping him a prisoner, to make arms, &c., for the tribe.

But, when Jewitt first came on deck, before his wound was attended to, the little sight that was left him, showed the blood of his murdered brethren, flowing over the boards, and the naked savages gathering round him in a circle, with their knives and daggers up, ready to strike.

They all united their clamorous voices, to have him despatched, so that there might be none left to tell the tale, whenever another vessel should come on their borders.

But the king would not consent to his death, till he had first examined and questioned him respecting what he would do, if spared.

In this trying moment, John felt, as he has since said, the value of having his Maker for a friend; and of having given up his life and all his interests into his Almighty care.

Maquina, wishing by his broken expressions, to make John understand that if he did not consent to his terms, he would be put to death, said to him,

'John—I speak—you no say no—you say no, daggers come!' He then asked if he would be his slave for life; if he would fight in his battles, make daggers and knives, and mend muskets for him; and many other similar questions, to all of which, John was careful to answer in such a way as to turn aside the dreaded wrath, and obtain leave to live.

When he had consented to all these proposals, Maquina told him he must now kiss his hands and feet, in token of perfect submission to him, as his future master and sovereign.

When John requested to have a tobacco leaf, of which there was plenty on board, bound on his wound, having long known its healing qualities, Maquina gave directions to have it brought, and taking the silk cravat from the neck of his patient, bound on the leaf with it, and fastened it round his head.

The air was very cold, and John was without his coat, which, together with his bodily suffering, and the awful spectacle before him, made him tremble like a poplar leaf.

Maquina saw this, and going below, brought up the Captain's great coat, and a bottle of rum, and throwing the coat over his shoulders, and putting the bottle to his mouth, he told him to drink, and he would not shiver so.

When John had followed this prescription, and was able to walk, the king led him to the quarter-deck, where he beheld a sight that chilled with horror, the blood that was left in his veins.

The trunkless heads of his unfortunate comrades, to the number of twenty-five, lay with their ghastly faces up, in a row before him; and not a sign of life appeared on board the ship, except in the persons of these dreadful executioners, and his own aching bosom.

One of the savages brought a head and asked whose it was. John told him it was the Captain's. Then another and another was shown, in the same way, till the horrid inspection of the whole number was gone through with, though some of the faces were so disfigured, as to make it impossible for the terrified survivor to tell to whom it had belonged.

The first cause of this dreadful sacrifice to revenge—the insult which Maquina felt he had received from the Captain, has already appeared to the reader; though the haughty red monarch did not see fit to explain it to Jewitt, till long after it took place.

The whole matter by which he justified himself in the merciless act, will be made known by some of the subsequent pages.

The slaughter, it seems, began while some of the seamen were busy in hoisting in the long-boat, when the savages on board, taking advantage of their situation, seized them and cut their throats with their own jack-knives.

Captain Salter was thrown overboard in the affray, but taken up and beheaded by the Indians in the canoes.

When the fatal work was over with those at the ship, the natives broke open the rum chest and magazine; and providing themselves with the deadly engines, went on shore in quest of the men that were there. When they had taken their lives, they severed their heads from their bodies, which

were all cast into the sea, and brought the appalling trophies to place them with those on board.

When John got able to stand, Maquina told him
he must get the ship round to Friendly Cove. To
do this, he cut the cables, and directed some of the
savages to go aloft and loose the sails.

Had it not been for the melancholy circumstances
that surrounded our disconsolate young friend,
he would have been much amused by the awk-
wardness of the Indians, at this new work of
handling the rigging of a vessel.

However, as the wind was exactly fair for the
purpose, they succeeded in running her into the
cove, and got her ashore on a sand beach, about
eight o'clock in the evening.

The king was welcomed home to the village, by
every mark of savage hilarity at his return, and
joy at his success, which could be shown by men,
women, and children.

Some ran to meet him, singing, leaping, and
shouting; while others made an almost insupporta-

ble din, to a head in such a state as John's must have been, by drumming with sticks on the sides and roofs of their houses, which were illuminated with blazing pine torches, stuck in the cracks, in honor of their king's return.

A sad, sad night was this to John, who, no doubt, while he now took his good father's advice, and resigned himself to the will of God, wished he had also taken it, and followed a better counsellor than his own romantic desire to see the world, before it was too late to be profited by it.

CHAPTER V.

John goes to the king's house—sees the women—gets acquainted with the young prince, Sat-sat-sok-sis—his supper—how he passes the night—he learns that one of the men is alive in the ship—finds it is Thompson—obtains permission for him to live.

Maquina's house, of which more will be said hereafter, was very large, and filled with people. The king had no less than nine wives; one of which was the mother of the young prince, the future heir to his honors.

This woman was very beautiful, and seemed to be a sort of queen over the others. She was the favorite of the king, and her son was his darling child.

The boy was about eleven years old. His name was *Sat-sat-sok-sis ;* but, this being rather an unwieldy word to manage, and as it may often occur in our narrative, we will abbreviate it, and in future call the prince Sat-sat.

John was conducted by Maquina to his house. The women came round the prisoner, and patting him softly on the head and shoulders, seemed to feel much pity for him in his sufferings, and manifested a great desire to do something to relieve the anguish of his wound.

Maquina called for something to eat, and his women brought him some dried clams and train-oil. He seated John beside him, and telling him to eat a good deal of oil, because it would make him *fat and strong*, began in earnest to show that his theory and practice agreed; at least, so far as gormandizing was concerned.

But, poor John! little would he have relished this disgusting repast, had there been no sorrow at his heart, as there was, swelling it almost to bursting.

Little, too, in his present state of feeling, could he have enjoyed the most sumptuous board that good old England ever offered him. But he made the best of his condition, knowing that to murmur would be in vain; and to show dissatisfaction might yet cost him his life.

During the time of supper, he heard the savages importuning their king to have him put to death; urging as a reason, that he might prevent other vessels from coming to trade with them, by informing, in some way, of what they had done.

But Maquina persisted in refusing to do this; saying that he had promised John his life, and he would not break his word. He again reminded them of the use he might be to them, by working at their arms, &c.

John had, also, to listen to their terrible boasting of what they had each done, in the murder of his companions; while, with horrid mimicry, they went through some of the most dreadful acts of the tragedy.

Sat-sat, the royal boy, attracted by curiosity, at the novel appearance of a white person, and in the dress that looked very odd to the little savage, came up to John to examine him.

John thought he might win the favor of the father, by securing that of the child; so he coaxed Sat-sat to come near, and caressed him till he got him willing to sit upon his knee.

He then cut the bright metal buttons from the coat he had on, and having run them on a string, fastened them round the neck of the child.

This greatly delighted his young majesty, who run off jingling his buttons, and showing them to the company with as much pride as a civilized lady would take in a necklace of pearls or diamonds.

And why should they not be as precious to him, as those more costly gems to their possessor? Nobody, it is true, had delved in the mine very deeply, or plunged into the ocean to obtain them.

Yet they were personal decorations, bright and pleasing to the eye, and they satisfied in him, the future monarch, that vain love for external show and ornament, which seems alike implanted in the bosom of the civilized and the savage, as well as the more expensive brilliants do those who, too often think more about them, than they do of obtaining the 'pearl of great price,' which our Savior recommends as the best of all treasures.

The thought of taking this method with Sat-sat, to win him, was a fortunate one for John. His buttons completely succeeded in purchasing the heart of the young prince, for their giver.

From that moment, Sat-sat attached himself to his new friend, acting out his human nature without reserve, upon the principle of those of whom Sat-sat had never heard, but who of old showed their self-interest, by seeking the 'loaves and fishes.'

When the hour came for those in the *Indian palace* to go to rest, the company stretched themselves on the ground; and John was made to lie down between Maquina and his son.

This, the king, who was much pleased with the attention he had shown to Sat-sat, told him, was to prevent the Indians, who seemed bent on taking his life, from coming to kill him in his sleep.

But the unfortunate youth, in his sadly new and strange condition, felt little inclination to sleep, notwithstanding his being literally in the bosom of the royal family.

About midnight, he heard one of the natives come and tell Maquina that there was a white man alive in the ship; and that he had been knocked down by him, in attempting to go on board.

When the Indian had retired, Maquina told John of this information, and said the white man must be slain in the morning.

John tried to dissuade him from his purpose; but he silenced his entreaties, and told him to lie down and go to sleep.

As Jewitt lay revolving the question in his mind, who this man might be, and by what means he could prevail on the king to let him live, he thought it was most probably Thompson, the sail-maker of the ship, as he had not recognised his head among those of the slain; and he remembered his having been below, at work on the sails, when the attack was made.

Thompson was a man about forty years of age; but as he had always lived a sea-faring life, from his boyhood, he looked much older. So John thought, that if it should prove to be he, who was alive, he would make Maquina think it was his father, and see if, on this account, he could not win mercy for him.

He fell into a doze towards morning; but at the rising of the sun, Maquina waked him, telling him he was going to the ship to kill the man, and that he must get up and go with him.

He obeyed in silence, and taking Sat-sat by the hand, led him out, following the father to the beach.

Here all the men of the tribe were assembled, waiting the approach of their king. When he came nigh, they gathered round him, listening with deep attention, while he informed them that there was a white man in the ship; and asked their general opinion whether he had better let him live, or have him put to death.

The natives expressed their united wishes that he might be kept alive, upon which John ventured to put in his plea.

He pointed to the boy, whom he still held by the hand, and asked Maquina if he loved his son; and being answered in the affirmative, he then asked the child if he loved his father. 'Yes,' was the reply. 'So do I love mine,' said he.

He threw himself now on his knees, at the feet of the king, entreating him to spare the life of his father, if it should prove to be he, who was in the vessel.

The heart of the savage was touched, at this pathetic appeal—he told John to rise and go on board the ship to tell the man to come out; and promised that if it was his father, he might live.

John went into the ship, and found to his great joy, that it was indeed Thompson, who was there alive and unhurt.

He was below when the massacre commenced, and finding that he had been unobserved by the natives, he hid himself in the hold, till all was over.

When the Indian came on board for plunder, in the night, thinking he was in quest of him. he

JEWETT PLEADING FOR THOMPSON.

determined to sell his life as dearly as possible, so he made a thrust at the savage and knocked him down; but he recovered himself in a moment, and springing up, ran off to tell the king.

John told Thompson, in as few words as possible, the plan he had laid to save his life, and the new relationship of father that he must assume—reminding him how careful he must be not to let the secret that he was not his father, be discovered by the sagacious Indians.

He then led him forth to Maquina, presenting him as his father, and promising to do every thing in his power to serve the natives, if they would spare his life.

But he assured them that, if they put his father to death, they would lose his services, however useful they might be in the way of his art of arms-making, &c., for he would certainly kill himself, as he could not bear this loss and live.

This was a powerful argument; and when Maquina recognised Thompson, and knew him to be the sail-maker, he thought his life, too, would be of service to them, in his employment, as he could make sails for their canoes; and reminding his people of this, at the same time, telling them that, by destroying him, they should lose the services of both; for he took John to be in earnest in his intention to kill himself, if Thompson was killed.

Thus, self-interest effected what humanity could not have done, with these barbarians; and it was agreed that the sail-maker's life should be spared.

Maquina then took both his prisoners to his house, and ordered something to be brought for them to eat; and John had the pleasure of seeing another entertainment of clams and train-oil set before him

CHAPTER VI.

The savages rob the ship of her contents, &c.—John secures the papers—two ships are seen—other tribes of natives come to Nootka—their reception—their supper, and a dance by Sat-sat —Maquina makes presents to his guests—their manner of receiving them—visitors continue to come and go.

THE two following days, the savages busied themselves in taking away the cargo of the ship, her sails, rigging, and what ever pleased their fancies, or promised to be in any way useful to them.

They even cut away her spars and masts, and turned her to a complete wreck.

The greatest part of the cargo, and all the most valuable articles, were carried to the king's house.

As John and his new father were obliged to assist in this work of depredation, they thought it a good opportunity to secure the ship's papers, &c., not knowing what way might offer for them to be of use; and as the natives set no value on such things, they met with little difficulty in taking them into their own possession.

John's chest had been broken open and plundered, but he still had the key; so he put into it the papers, with the Captain's writing-desk, a blank account-book that he found, and which he thought might serve him, as he knew not how long he should remain in captivity, for to keep some little accounts of what he might meet with.

In the desk were some writing materials, which he hoped to be allowed to use; and he also found a Bible and Prayer Book, from which he expected great consolation.

These articles, with a few small tools, he found no difficulty in securing in his chest, in which he also put a journal that had been kept by the mate, and some drawings owned by him, which he reserved for his friends, in case of there ever being an opportunity to convey them to the places of their abode.

On the twenty-sixth, two ships hove in sight; and, while their appearance filled the bosoms of the captives with hope and joy, at least, for a short time, it threw the natives into great consternation, for they thought they were coming to punish them for the work of destruction they had been doing.

They had immediate recourse to their newly-acquired arms and ammunition, and kept up a brisk firing, till the ships, not disposed to be peppered with hot shot, returned a few rounds, that did no harm, and stood out to sea again; thus drowning the hopes of poor John and his fellow-captive, in the wide-spread ocean, over whose surface they cut their watery way, till out of sight.

These ships, as was afterwards ascertained, were the Mary, and the Juno, of Boston, Massachusetts.

When the ships were out of sight, Maquina began to express great regret that he had let his people fire at them, as he feared that others, hearing of this hostile treatment, would be prevented from coming to trade with them.

Not many days after the capture of the ship, the

news having spread round among the different tribes of natives on the coast, brought them in hosts to Nootka.

There came canoes filled with savages, of at least twenty tribes, from the north and south, who hastened to pay Maquina a visit of gratulation for his success, and expecting, at the same time, to better themselves by the presents it is the custom of these people to bestow on their guests on such an occasion.

Among these visitors, many belonged to the tribes of the north, that were tributary to the Nootka.

But those who were the best dressed, and sailed in the most neatly-finished canoes, belonged to the *Wickanninish*, a large and powerful tribe of the south.

These had come the distance of two hundred miles, which, with sails to their canoes, and a good breeze, they performed in twenty-four hours.

An odd and ludicrous scene was presented on the beach as the canoes of the visitors approached it; for, Maquina, proud of his new acquisition, set out to welcome his guests in what he thought real European gentility of style.

And a motley group did the natives of Nootka form as they assembled on the beach, clad in their new and ill-gotten gear, which had been taken from the ship.

Some had on *kutsacks*, or cloaks, made of broad-cloths of blue, red, and yellow; with stockings drawn over their heads, while, about their necks were hung powder-horns, shot-bags, and cartouch boxes; and many had eight or ten muskets apiece on their shoulders, and half a dozen daggers fastened in one girdle.

Many articles of clothing they did not know how to wear, and they put them on in a manner to make most grotesque figures of themselves.

Equipped in this way, they all squatted upon the beach, holding their muskets perpendicularly, with the butts resting on the sand, waiting orders to fire the salute.

The cannon had been taken from the ship to the

beach, and laid upon two sticks of timber; and at these, Thompson was stationed; while Maquina had taken a stick and a trumpet, and gone up on the roof of his house, where he set up such a drumming on the roof, with his stick, it was enough to stun any but a savage head.

When the canoes drew up to the shore, he spoke through his trumpet, telling his subjects to fire.

At the word of command, they obeyed, but fearfully and awkwardly, keeping in their squat position, and pressing the butt of the gun, as before, hard upon the ground.

At the same moment, Thompson fired the cannon, upon which the natives threw themselves back, and tumbled and rolled about as if they had been shot.

Then they sprang up, and ran and danced about upon the beach, singing a song of triumph, and boasting of their exploits; while the strange, wild sounds of their voices were accompanied by such savage gesticulations as were sometimes laughable, and sometimes frightful.

When this ceremony was over, the king came down from his perch, to meet his guests, and invite them in, to partake of the royal entertainment that had been prepared for them in his house.

This was a large quantity of whale blubber, smoked herring-spawn, and dried fish with train-oil, that were set before the company in large trays, placed upon the ground, the floor of the red monarch's palace.

When the feast was over, and the trays removed, preparations were made for the dance, which was to close the entertainment.

Three of the principal chiefs, clad in otter-skin mantles, a dress which they only assumed on great occasions, and having their heads newly powdered with white down, came forward into the room, bearing each a bag of white down, similar to that upon their heads, and began to scatter it round, so as to represent a fall of snow.

This, I think a pretty idea, and quite a delicate one too, as it was strewing the way, with this soft and beautiful material, for the young prince to step upon.

It is a thought of a more refined nature than that which, a short time before, had occasioned the blubber and the sperm to be placed in trays upon the same spot.

Behind these chiefs, who came paving the way in so gentle and soft a manner, followed Sat-sat, with a long piece of yellow cloth, wrapped loosely about him; and tricked out with small bells, a cap, and a mask in the form of a wolf's head.

Behind him came the king himself, in a robe of sea-otter skin, and having in his mouth a small whistle, while in his hand he held a rattle, which he shook to keep time to a wild, fantastic tune that he played upon his whistle.

When they had passed, with great gravity and order, round the apartment, each was seated, except Sat-sat, who immediately commenced his dance.

This dance he performed chiefly by taking a

squat position, and thus, springing up as far as he had power to go; and incessantly turning round upon his heels in a very small circle, and with great swiftness in his motion.

The dance, with only a few intervals for him to take breath, Sat-sat kept up for two hours, to the doleful music which the chiefs made, by drumming with short sticks, on pieces of plank, the under side of which had been scooped out into a hollow, so as to sound the louder, and the more like a hollow instrument.

During the dance, Maquina and his chiefs continued singing; and the women uttered their plaudits at every extraordinary jump of the young performer, crying out, at the top of their voices, ' *Wocash! Wocash! Tyee!*' (good! very good! prince.)

When the dance was ended, Maquina began to deal out gifts to the strangers, in the name of his son Sat-sat.

These presents consisted of pieces of cloth, about

two yards long, that had been taken from the ship, muskets, powder, shot, &c.

Maquina, on this occasion, gave away four hundred yards of cloth, one hundred muskets, as many looking-glasses, and twenty casks of powder, besides many other articles.

The manner in which these people received the gifts, was very odd, and such as seemed very uncivil and ungracious.

When the king held out the gift, the receiver snatched it from him rudely, and with as stern a look as could be put on, saying at the same time, '*Wocash, Tyee!*'

John thought by their looks, that all were dissatisfied with their presents; but he afterwards learnt that this stern expression was considered among the savages a mark of respect; and it was viewed as a great indignity to have it omitted on the reception of a thing bestowed; especially, if the giver was a person in authority.

After the presents were distributed, Maquina

insisted on all the strangers, but the chiefs, going on board their canoes to sleep, to prevent their pillaging during the night; and he set John and Thompson, armed with cutlasses and pistols, to watch them. The chiefs were accommodated with a place in the houses.

The natives of the different tribes along the coast continued to come in this way, to Nootka, for several days, bringing with them such sorts of provisions as would be acceptable, and receiving in return, presents from Maquina; after which, they went directly back to their homes.

CHAPTER VII.

The ship is burnt—many articles lost by the fire—some valuable things saved—Maquina discovers a tierce of rum among his spoils—invites company—holds a carousal—all get intoxicated —John empties the rum-cask upon the ground—anecdote of a merchant—John begins to work at his trade—he assists Thompson in getting food.

On the morning of the eighteenth, John and his companion in bondage witnessed a spectacle which was to them a sad sight, while it shone brightly before them.

As they arose, early in the morning, and went out, on looking towards the ship, they saw her wrapped in flames. She had taken fire by means of some sparks that some of the natives who went on board in the night, for plunder, had let fall into the hold, among the light combustibles, which soon broke out into a blaze, and entirely completed the destruction of the only trace of a civilized country, except the articles carried on shore, which appeared to their sight.

Besides, there were a great many provisions still on board, which they had hoped to take out for their own use and comfort, as the natives would not touch a thing that had any flavor of salt, and there were many other articles that would have been left to their enjoyment, as they were as offensive to the savage taste, as the whale blubber and train-oil were to theirs.

But it was a splendid, though melancholy sight to them, to see the Boston, as she lay upon the edge of the great waters, that spread themselves out so far on one side, and the border of a savage land, that stretched off on the other, beyond the power of their imaginations to follow. It was, I say, a melancholy sight to see her thus standing between these two elements, for a third, and more terrible one to devour her.

As the flames towered high above the water, they waved and sported on the surrounding air, as the

THE SHIP BOSTON IN FLAMES.

plumes of a group of soldiers are tossed and played with by the winds that pass.

The captives breathed out their farewell to the unfortunate ship as she became a mass of living coals, and then crumbled to pieces before their eyes.

The natives, too, seemed very sorry for the loss, as there were many things still about her, which they had intended to save.

John lost his anvil and bellows, which had not been removed to the beach; though nearly all the other things with which he worked, were saved.

Among the things that had been carried on shore, he was glad to find a nautical almanac, which one of the natives gave him; and a case of port wine, and a box of chocolate, both of which, as the Indians did not like their taste, fell to the disposal of John and Thompson.

The almanac, John expected, would be of great use to him in determining on points of time; and the natives, in their turn, were highly delighted, when examining their booty, about two days after the burning of the ship, they found among a variety of things, a cask of rum, and a case of gin.

Since their intercourse with the whites, who first introduced ardent spirits among the American Indians, they have become very fond of the '*fire-water*,' as they used to call rum, when they first began to use it.

It was nearly night when Maquina discovered that he had such a prize in his possession, and much elated with the anticipated enjoyment of his intoxicating draught, he invited all the men to a feast at his house, or, to use a more fashionable term, to an *evening party*, to enjoy with him the fire-water.

The native Indians of Virginia, when they obtained a bag of gunpowder from some of the early settlers, never having seen any thing of the kind before, but finding it a thing of great power, as well as pretty and curious in its effects, put it aside, to plant with their corn, as they said they wanted to become acquainted with 'that kind of seed.'

But Maquina knew better than to pour his

treasure into the ground, to see if it would produce little rivulets or fountains of that kind of water; so when the company had assembled and partaken of the feast and the beverage, they soon grew so intoxicated and wild, that John and Thompson fled to the woods for safety, and the women made their escape to other houses for the night.

The men only were engaged in this drinking frolic, the women of Nootka being perfectly temperate, and never using anything but water, by way of drink.

About midnight, when the wild shouts and frightful sounds of the savage mirth had died away, the captives, feeling desirous of knowing what was going on at the *palace*, returned to look into the state of affairs in and about the premises.

The Indians, after their carousal, overcome by the effects of the strong draughts they had taken, were all stretched out on the ground, in profound sleep, or stupefaction, such as follows excessive drinking.

It had now been an easy thing for the captives

to destroy their lives, or bind them down, had there been any vessel to which they might flee for refuge.

But to kill the poor untutored savages, was a thing that was not to be thought of; and to make any other attempt upon them, would have been useless, as there was no possible way of escape by water, and to go back into the woods would only be exposing themselves to the hostilities of other natives; so they thought the best thing they could do, would be to prevent the danger of another fire-water jubilee.

John went to the rum-cask, and, finding it had still enough in it to make its effects dreaded, he took a small gimblet, and bored in the under side of the cask, a hole large enough to let the spirit take its own way and its own time to sink into the earth, before morning.

He had the satisfaction to find, that in a few hours, the soil had drunk up, what the children of the soil had left; and that there remained no more an opportunity for the natives to have another frolic of this sort.

And he now saw that the burning of the ship, which he had before regretted so much, was a wise direction of Providence; as there was on board a large quantity of rum, which, had it been secured by the natives, would have been a source of great trouble to him and Thompson, if it did not cause their death.

John's act in the *temperance cause* reminds me of an anecdote, which, as I was knowing to the facts at the time, I will digress from our story, to relate.

In the summer of 1832, a merchant of Newburyport, Massachusetts, having long been convinced of the evil of furnishing the seamen who went out in his vessels, with a supply of spirituous liquor, for their voyage, began to consider seriously on the easiest and best way to dispose of a couple of hogsheads of rum that had been a great while in his store.

To sell it to others, he felt, would not be destroying the evil, but only passing it off on his neighbors—he had too much conscience for this.

To ship the rum to some other port, would only be removing from his sight the bad consequences which he felt certain would follow the use of it.

So he called a truckman, and directed him to take the hogsheads of rum on his trucks, and carry them to the head of the wharf. He then bored a hole in the head of each, and let them empty their contents into the Merrimac river.

Had he sold the rum, it would have brought him much money; but in this act, he gave a proof that a man of sound principle will be ready to make a personal sacrifice of worldly gain, to the cause of general good; and that he will not countenance or assist others in doing what he would deem it wrong for himself to do.

We will now resume our story. John had so far recovered from the hurt on his head, and the shock he had sustained in the loss of his friends, as to be able to begin to work a little.

He found a large flat stone, which he converted into an anvil; and heating the metal on which he

worked, in a common fire, for a furnace, he commenced his business, much to the satisfaction of the
king and his wives.

For the women he made bracelets and other ornaments of copper and steel, which pleased them
highly; and for the men, he mended their arms,
&c., which won for him their favor, also; and they
began to think they had a valuable prize in their
young captive.

The neighboring tribes of Indians still kept flock-
ing to Nootka, with their stores of provisions, to
exchange for a share of the spoils of the ship; and
John was allowed to make, *on his own hook*, some
small ornamental articles which he sold to them,
for either victuals for himself and Thompson, or
pieces of European cloth, and wearing apparel,
which they had just received from his master.

I speak of John's procuring food in this way,
because it is the habit of the Nootka Indians to
make the most of to-day, and let to-morrow take
care of itself; and they would often destroy, at one
of their feasts, what would have kept them com-

fortable for several days, though they afterwards had to take a very short allowance, in consequence of their careless waste.

John generally fared as well as his master's family; but Thompson, who could not bring his spirit into subjection to his new lords, being of an irritable temper, often manifested a state of feeling towards the Indians, that made him no favorite with them, and greatly displeased them.

He would frequently have had to go hungry, had not his adopted son procured food for him, either by selling his work, or by begging for him of others, who did not belong to the king's family.

John was so highly esteemed in the village, that when he did not find enough of such disgusting fare as he had to live on, at home, he could go into any hut where he saw a smoke, (the sign that they were cooking,) and get something, which was readily given him for himself and his friend; thus getting hunger satisfied with what did not do much towards delighting the taste.

CHAPTER VIII.

John's remarks about cooking—Maquina throws away the kettle of salt—John's head gets better—Thompson's history—he strikes Sat-sat—an affray, in which he is likely to be slain— John pleads till the king consents to his life being spared— strawberries appear—John begins his journal.

It would have been a cause of great pleasure to the captives, could they have had permission to cook their salmon, halibut, and other food in their own way, which they might easily have done with the pot and other cooking utensils, that had been saved from the ship, had not Maquina forbidden it.

He and all the rest of the tribe were so proud and tenacious of their own manner of cooking, that whenever John procured a fish, he was obliged to give it up to the women, and let them make what sort of a mess they pleased with it, and it generally came out a pretty unpalatable dish.

Once, when the prisoners went away by themselves, into a retired place, in order to boil down some sea-water, to make salt for their food, Maquina, discovering what they were about, was so offended, that he spilt their brine, and threw the kettle into the sea.

This act was not because Maquina wished to treat John unkindly—on the contrary, he seemed disposed to show him much kindness, in his barbarous way; but he was so proud, he could not bear anything like innovation, or like dissatisfaction with their mode of living.

Once, as a great favor, he permitted John to cook a salmon; and he and his favorite wife condescended to taste of it; but they did not like it, and turned to that which was done according to their own fashion.

The wound on John's head was now getting well fast. The tobacco having been brought on shore, allowed him a fresh leaf every day, which was the only thing applied to the cut, besides the water with which it was washed, and some loaf-sugar that the king gave him once, to take out the proud flesh that had formed.

Sat-sat's mother would often point to John's forehead, and giving a piteous look, express a wish to have it well; while Maquina seemed also to feel much compassion for him, and spared him what labor he could, asking frequently if his head pained him.

But Thompson, who could not help showing by his rude manner and unbending spirit, that he could not well brook his captivity and subjection to his red masters, was not much in favor with any of the natives.

To account a little for the rough outside and the stubborn spirit of Thompson, it may be well to say a few words about his origin and life.

He was born in Philadelphia; but he ran away from his friends when a very small boy, and entered as cabin-boy in a ship bound to London. When he arrived at London, not knowing what to do with himself, which is often, I suspect, the case

with boys as disobedient and wayward as he, he
went and engaged himself as an apprentice to a
collier.

He was afterwards impressed on board an English man-of-war, and remained about twenty-seven
years in the service of the British navy.

During this time, he had encountered many pe-
rils, and engaged in some hot battles. He was a
strong, muscular man, and an expert boxer. He
had been so familiar with danger, it had lost its
dread to him; and whenever his temper was raised,
he was wholly regardless of his own life.

This daring spirit he could not, or would not,
overcome; and it came very near proving fatal to
him, in his new situation.

The Indians, it seems, had taken the lamps from
the ship, and placed them in the king's room, instead of the pine torches with which it was before
lighted; and it fell to Thompson's lot to fill and
light them.

One evening, when John was at the house of

one of the chiefs, about some work he was doing for him, word was brought him, that Maquina was going to kill Thompson.

He dropped his work, and running to see what was the matter, he found Maquina holding a loaded musket, while he foamed at the mouth with rage, at Thompson, who stood before him with his bosom bare, telling him to fire.

He stepped between them, and addressing the king in the most soothing words and tones, entreated him to spare his father, and at length prevailed on him to let him take the musket, and to sit down.

When the incensed monarch grew a little cool, John learned the cause of the offence.

Thompson was about filling the lamps, when a throng of Indian boys, eager to see how it was done, gathered round him, pulling his clothes and annoying him in various ways, till they made him spill the oil.

Upon this, he flew into a passion, and gave the

first boy that he could lay his hand on, a blow in the face that knocked him down.

This happened to be Sat-sat, and the act of striking him the savages regarded as the highest indignity, as the persons of the royal family are held sacred; and the sensation produced among them, at seeing their little prince's majesty thus profaned, cannot be conceived of by one who did not witness it.

When Maquina saw his son's face covered with blood, he had resolved at once on taking the life of the offender; and with this intent he had seized the musket, which, had not John arrived at that moment, would have laid Thompson breathless before him.

It was a long time before Maquina could be appeased; and for a great while after this affray, he would say, now and then, ' John, *you* die—Thompson kill.'

But the king was not all who was to be pacified —the whole tribe felt themselves ill-treated in the

person of their young prince. They held a council, and it was resolved upon, that Thompson
should be put to death in the most cruel manner.

But John assuring the king that, if he delivered
his father over to be tormented and slain by his
people, he would certainly not survive him, but
would destroy his own life; thus prevailed on him
to forbid their injuring him, in the least, which, he
took good care to inform John, was on his account,
not on his father's.

Sat-sat also assured him of this, afterwards; for
he said, if that blow had come on him from any
one of the natives, it would have caused him who
gave it, to be put to death at once.

Yet, strange as it may seem, the difficulty thus
brought on Thompson, by giving way to anger, did
not teach him much prudence.

He detested the Indians, and he did not try to
conceal his feelings towards them. This often
brought him into a squabble with some one of
them, and gave great anxiety to his fellow-captive.

He used to say sometimes that he abhorred the

natives so much, he would rather die, than live a slave among them, after being the brave soldier that he had been, and fighting the French and the Spaniards as he had done.

This irritable disposition of Thompson's kept John in constant fear, lest he should, by some violence or insulting act, forfeit his life, and cause him to be left to bear the horrors of his bondage alone.

It was now about the middle of May. The climate was so mild, and the season so fine, that the strawberries, with which the coast abounded, were fully ripe.

It was a great luxury to the captives to gather these, and eat them fresh from the spot where they grew; but the natives would not use them without a dressing of the nauseous train-oil.

About this time, Thompson, who could not write himself, importuned John, frequently, to begin his journal; and told him, as he had no ink, he would cut his own finger and let him have blood from it to write with, whenever he wished to set anything down.

But John was spared the painful acceptance of so strange an offer; as he found a kind of wild berry, the juice of which, being boiled with powdered charcoal, and filtered through a cloth, made very good ink.

He prepared a bottle or two of this, and gathering up some of the raven and crow-quills, that were scattered about the shore, he furnished himself with a clam-shell for an inkstand, and thus provided, he began his regular diary, about the first of June.

CHAPTER IX.

*John's conduct towards the natives—Thompson's—his second
insult to a Tyee—description of Nootka—its buildings—Dexter's images.*

JOHN had, from the first of his bondage, resolved
on using a mild, conciliatory deportment towards
the natives; and to set about learning their language as fast as possible, so as to understand them,
and express himself in the safest terms, as this he
considered the surest way to win their favor, and
lessen the pains of captivity.

But it was far otherwise with Thompson. He
insisted that he did not want to know the language
of so detestable a race, and declared that he would
not defile his mouth with their lingo.

It was not long after his thrust at Sat-sat, that
he got himself and his friend into a similar affair

of danger by striking the son of a chief, for calling him a *white slave.*

The Indian lad was eighteen years old; an age, which, by the custom of the tribe, endowed him with the honors and the dignity of a *Tyee*, (chief.)

But John, making use of all his address, succeeded a second time in extricating the white offender from the entanglement into which his own folly and rashness had brought him, and which made all the tribe clamorous for his death.

It seemed to be Thompson's determination *not* to learn wisdom by experience, but rather to 'eat of the fruit of his own ways, and be filled with his own devices.'

It may now be well, as we may not find a more convenient stopping-place in our narrative, to pause here a little while, and suspend the thread of the story, to give a short description of the place with which it is connected, and an account of the customs of the people who inhabited it.

The village of Nootka was situated in between

forty-nine and fifty degrees of north latitude, at the bottom of Friendly Cove, on the north-west side.

The houses, or huts, of which it consisted when John was a prisoner there, were about twenty in number, and stood upon the slope of a small hill that rose gradually up from the border of the beach.

Friendly Cove, formed between the line of coast on the one side, and a point of land that extends three leagues into the sound, on the other, is between a quarter and a half of a mile wide, and from a half to three quarters of a mile long. It is a small harbor, and affords a good anchorage for ships coming close to the shore.

The eastern and western shores of this harbor are abrupt and rugged, with trees growing close to the water's edge; but at the bottom of the cove, to the north-west, there is a fine sandy beach, the same on which I have described the natives as sitting with their guns up, to hail their visitors with a salute.

From the village there stretches off to the north and north-east, a strip of plain, the soil of which is soft and rich; but it soon terminates at the sea-coast, that is lined with reefs of rocks that make it impossible for vessels to approach the shore. The coast in the neighborhood of Nootka is rather low, and not much diversified with hills and dales. It abounds with fine clear streams of sweet water, and the soil is good, and overspread with noble forests of pine, spruce, beech, and other trees.

A few years previous to the time of our story, the Spaniards, thinking the hill where the village of Nootka stood, would afford them a fine situation for a garrison, took possession of it, driving the Indians back several miles into the woods, and demolishing their houses.

But when the Spanish garrison was expelled by the English, the Indians returned with great joy to their favorite spot, and rebuilt their town.

When John was there, the foundation of the Spanish governor's house was still visible, and there were several kinds of European plants, such as peas, turnips, and onions, that had scattered themselves about in the soil and were growing, though in a stinted manner, without cultivation.

The houses at Nootka, which I have already said, were about twenty in number, were of various sizes, according to the rank of the Tyees who lived in them, as each house contained several families, over whom the chief who occupied it with them, was considered the rightful lord.

Each family held their little allotment in the house, separate from the other parts; and each house was large enough to accommodate a great many people—none being too small for two families.

These buildings, of which Maquina's was the largest, stood nearly in a direct line, thus forming by one range, the little village on the hill's side.

The manner in which the Nootkans built, was as follows: and it does not seem quite so difficult as getting the materials ready for use, which must in their way, and with their means, have been a very laborious process.

When a building was to be erected, and the preparations were made, the first step was to set two large posts so far into the ground as to make them sure to stand, and at such a distance from each other, as to comprise the length of the house—the top of each post being hollowed out, so as to let the end of a spar fit in and remain secure.

An immensely large and long spar was then laid upon them to form the ridgepole of the house; but if the length of the house required it, two additional posts were set up, so as to admit of the ridgepole being formed of two spars, which was not unfrequently the case, as the houses were some of them very long.

The king's house was one hundred feet long, and the single spar that passed from end to end of it, measured eight feet four inches in circumference.

The corner posts were to be set up next, marking the width of the house; but they were shorter than those on which the ridgepole rested, so as to have another spar placed on each side of the first, and a little lower, to give a slant to the roof of the house.

The spars that were to come under the eaves of the building, were made flat on the upper side, with a little rising edge left on the outer part, to prevent the planks, of which the covering of the house was to be made, from sliding off.

When these side spars were laid on the posts, the builders proceeded to laying on the roof. The planks of which this was formed, were heavy, with a broad feather-edge so as to lap; and placed one end on the ridgepole, the other on the side beam, closely lapped along, till one coat of the roof was formed.

Another coat of planks was laid on so as to jut over the eaves, or, beyond the ends of the first laying, in a way to exclude the rain entirely.

These were only fastened on by large rocks that were laid upon them; but they were often so insecure as to oblige the men to go out and sit upon the roofs of their houses, in a violent storm, to keep them from being blown away.

It seems to be reversing the common order of things, to be sure, for a man to have to shelter, or protect his house, instead of receiving protection from it in a storm; but so it was with these poor, uncivilized, untutored savages, who knew no better way of fastening their buildings together.

A missionary among the Sandwich Islands, informs us that some of the natives set so high a value on common nails, that when they have obtained a few from some vessel, they have been known to plant them, in order to have a tree come up and bear nails, not knowing how else they could be produced.

But the Nootkans had no nails to spring up from their grounds, and if, in any other way, they had been furnished with enough for their buildings, it is doubtful whether they would have condescended to use them, so proud and tenacious were they of their own way in everything.

To form the side of the house, a double row of stancheons was set up, as high as the eaves, the distance of each pair from the other, about as long as the planks to be used, and the stakes of each couple, just far enough apart to admit the width of the plank.

The planks were then slidden in between them, resting one upon the edge of the other, till the side of the building was sealed up.

There was but one entrance to the house, and this commonly at the end; though that of Maquina's house was in the middle of the side.

They had no chimneys, or fire-places, but a few stones put together to build the fire on, and a board in the roof above it, so fixed as to be shoved aside, whenever they made a fire, and wanted to let the smoke out.

Through the middle of the building, there runs along from end to end, a passage about eight feet wide, on each side of which lived numerous families, without any partition to mark their limits, but all having their separate fire-places, furniture, &c.

The earth formed the only floor of these odd habitations, and the only bed of their occupants, except a piece of bark matting which they spread down, and upon which they laid themselves to rest, with only their clothing thrown over them for a covering.

The ridgepole of the king's house was painted in alternate red and black rings, and the tops of the posts were rudely carved and painted so as to represent the heads of men of an enormous size.

This was done by way of embellishment to the palace, and to distinguish the royal abode from that of a subject.

A taste and a whim similar to that of the Indian monarch, seems to have actuated the late noted Timothy, (alias Lord,) Dexter, who, some thirty years ago, or thereabouts, caused to be placed over the arched door-way, and in the front yard of his spacious house in Newburyport, Massachusetts, numerous carved and painted images, clothed in military, or other professional attire, that stood up as large as life, on double rows of high pillars, each labeled with a name, such as '*Washington,*' '*Hancock,*' '*Adams,*' &c.

A few of these images remain to this day, the ridiculous and weather-beaten monuments of the folly of him whose mortal form has crumbled, long before them, into dust.

CHAPTER X.

How they made boards at Nootka—their furniture—their man-
ner of eating—their feasts—how they made cloth—their dress.

THE manner in which the Nootkans prepared their planks for building, was by splitting them out from large pine logs, which they did with hard wooden wedges, and then reducing them to a proper thickness by working on them with their chisels.

This was a labor that required much time and patience, and the Indians must have obtained, not only their food, but also their dwellings, by 'the sweat of the brow.'

Their houses were, none of them, more than ten feet high, at the ridgepole, but, broad and long as they were, they must have cost many a hard day's work, with their boards procured by so slow and toilsome a process.

John found that the furniture of one of these

houses consisted neither in pieces of porcelain, alabaster, marble, polished mahogany, or gilt-work; and that the royal establishment did not differ from the others in its household gear.

All that these people seemed to want was just enough for use; and for this, very little sufficed.

They had boxes in which to keep their clothes, furs, and other articles which they wished to preserve most carefully, formed of pine, and very smooth, with covers to shut closely over and fastened on by flexile twigs, instead of hinges and locks.

Sometimes these boxes were ornamented with rows of small white shells, that were brought up from the sea in so curious a way, that I shall hereafter describe it.

With baskets for their dried fish, and other purposes, and bags of the bark matting, of which they also had a patch to sleep upon, the Indians had tubs of an oblong square, and of various sizes, from six feet by four, down to a very small measure.

These tubs they used, too, for keeping their soft

provisions, for cooking, and many other uses. They were formed by the chisel from square blocks.

Their dishes were only large trays, formed in a similar manner, and about three feet long, one wide, and eight inches deep.

Around one of these trays, filled with whatever their meal happened to consist of, whether of stewed salmon, whale-blubber, herring-spawn, or something else as inviting, from four to six persons generally seated themselves, on the ground, with their legs crossed and bent under them, to partake of the repast.

They used nothing but their hands in eating, unless the dish chanced to be a soup, or swimming with oil; in which case, each resorted to a clam-shell as a vehicle to convey to his mouth, the aliment that might otherwise have slipped through his fingers.

Their food consisted chiefly of fish of various kinds, clams, muscles, and a variety of wild berries, all of which, even to the delicate strawberries and raspberries, had to take a dressing of train-oil, before they were eaten.

One way which the Nootkans had to cook a fish was this: They put into the largest tub, water enough to make their broth, and heating stones very hot, put them into the water till it boiled.

Then they cut off the head, tail, and fins of a salmon, and laid the fish in the water which was kept boiling by the stones from the fire, till the whole become thickened by the decomposed salmon; and then it was taken out to be eaten, in a sort of unseasoned soup. This was with them a favorite mess.

Another mode of their cooking was by steam. This was done by building a large fire, upon which a layer of stones was placed, which becoming well heated through, were overspread with green leaves and pine boughs. Upon these the fish, muscles, clams, &c., were put and covered closely with a mat, to confine the steam, till the cooking was done.

In this way, the prisoners found the clams and

muscles were well done and tasted very good, and the salmon was better than that done after the other fashion.

They seldom cooked their food at Nootka in any other than these two ways, though they sometimes roasted herring and sprats, by spitting them on a stick which they stuck into the ground, and built a fire round it. The roe of salmon they supported over the fire between the ends of two split pieces of pine, till it was roasted.

At their meals, the king and chiefs had separate trays, from which no one except the queen, or principal wife of the chief, was allowed to eat.

But whenever the king or one of the chiefs wished to confer a great mark of favor on one of the people, he would call him to him and give him some choice morsel from his tray.

The slaves, of which there were many, in the village that had been captured from other tribes, in time of war, fared as well as their masters, eating at the same time, and of the same food, but only feeding from separate trays.

Whenever a feast, or a *party*, was given by a king or a chief, a master of ceremonies was chosen, who conducted the whole with great decorum and style.

He received the guests as they entered the house, and pointed out to each his place with much exactness and perfect order, as rank and standing were strictly attended to on such occasions, and no one was allowed to take a seat without regard to these.

This etiquette, as well as many other usages of these people concerning their dress and entertainments, one might almost view as a prophetical burlesque upon the refined ways of civilized life at a more modern date.

Invitations to these feasts were often given to all the people of the village; and in making preparations for it, a great quantity of food was cooked up to waste. Excessive eating was a condition to be complied with at one of these parties.

He who gormandized the most was considered as enjoying the entertainment most highly, while the host felt that the height of his felicity depended on the height of the heaps of stewed fish, herring-spawn, blubber, clams, &c., that he should set before his guests.

It was the custom, when one of these entertainments was over, for each one of the company to convey to his own house, all the food that remained in his tray, after he had eaten what he could. The king and the chiefs gave the contents of their trays to their slaves, to be carried home for them; but the others took each his portion of the remains of the feast, and managed to get home with it as well as he could.

John and his companion made pretty awkward work at first, in this kind of business; and they felt very oddly carrying home, at arms-length, the boiled fish and other food that they had received where they visited.

But they soon became accustomed to it, and were very glad of what they could get in this way.

The manner in which these Indians prepared the bark of trees, of which they made their cloth, mats, baskets, &c., was to soak it first, a fortnight, and then beat it between a block fixed for the purpose, and an instrument of bone, or hard wood, till all the brittle, crumbly part was separated from the fine fibrous parts, and left it soft and flexible, in fine, long threads, quite even and delicate.

These threads they parceled out, rolling each bunch under the hand till it became closely combined in a little cord, and when a sufficient number of these cords were made, they were laid close together, and a thread strong enough to hold them fast to each other, interwoven among them, somewhat in the way that our rush and cane window-shades are made.

This web formed the cloth of which the common people at Nootka made their dresses, and many other articles.

If they wished to have their cloth variegated, they stained the threads with the juice of berries, or something else, before they were woven.

Some of the dresses were painted with red ochre, the better to keep out the rain.

One garment generally constituted the dress, and

this was a sort of cloak or mantle, which they called *kutsack*—the form I have before described.

The bottoms of some of these dresses were painted, and some ornamented with a border of sea-otter skin, or a kind of gray cloth made of the hair of some animal which was obtained from the tribes farther at the south.

In the winter, they wore an additional garment, when they went out. This was a sort of hood, with a place so formed as to admit the head; and large enough to come down behind over the shoulders; and before, over the breast. It was trimmed all round with a border of fur.

The chiefs had kutsacks of sea-otter skin; but these were only worn on great occasions. They had also cloaks of the skin of a large animal, which was brought to them by the Wickanninish tribe.

This skin was so dressed as to be left in its perfect form, but with all the hair taken off in a way that showed the skin white and soft as deer-skin, but twice as thick.

When the skin was dressed, they painted it with

figures of various kinds, representing human heads, moons, fishes, canoes, and many other devices.

They called the name of this skin *Metamelth.* It was apparently from an animal of the moose kind.

The Indians prized it, or a dress of it, very highly, and considered it too precious to be put on, except when they wanted to make the greatest display; it was, therefore, considered as the war-dress of a king or chief.

Strips of this skin were cut and painted for girdles, borders for their cloaks, and bracelets for their wrists and ankles.

The dress of the females differed very little from that of the men. The chief dissimilarity between them was, that the kutsack of the female was so long as to reach the feet, and fastened close under the chin; while that of the men was tied loosely on one shoulder, and reached only below the knee.

When they went out on any excursion, particularly when whaling was the object, they wore a sort of cap, made of their cloth, in the form of a sugar-loaf, with the point taken off, so as to make the top flat.

A strip of the metamelth skin, ornamented with rows of small white shells, was attached to it as a tassel.

The caps of the common people were painted red; but those of the chiefs were diversified with various colors. The one worn by the king, the *crown imperial*, was larger than the others, and on the top, had an ornament in form of an urn, to finish it off.

In the front was painted a canoe, with a harpooner, in the prow, aiming, and ready to strike at a whale. The other parts of the cap were laid in plaits of alternate black and white. They called this cap, *Seeya-pocks*.

CHAPTER XI

*Description of the Nootkans—their habit of painting ornaments—
manner of fishing for Ife-maw—continuation of remarks on
their personal decorations &c.—nose jewels.*

THE personal appearance of the Indians of Nootka was found by our young hero more agreeable to
the eye than that of any other tribes that he saw.

They were well formed, straight, robust and
strong. The greatest defect in their proportions,
was in their legs and feet, and this seemed rather the
work of habit than of nature ; as it arose probably
from their mode of sitting upon the feet, with the
legs bent under them, which gave them a heavy,
clumsy look.

When not disguised by paint, their faces, of a
coppery hue, and an oval form, were fine and in-
telligent.

Their eyes, bright and black, were rather small ;—

the nose neither flat nor too prominent;—their lips thin and the teeth very sound and white. Their hair was long, black and coarse. Their beards were all plucked out by the roots, bearing no sign of one, but making the faces smooth, among all the men but the king, who had let his grow uncut, upon the upper lip, in a mustachio, as a mark of royal dignity and distinction.

The stature of the men was generally about five feet, and from six to eight inches in height. But one man of dwarfish growth, being the only instance of the kind that John saw, was thirty years old, and only three feet, three inches high. He was, however, well proportioned, and in good health.

The women were much lighter in their complexions than the men; many of them not being darker than the women in some parts of the South of Europe. They were very modest in their deportment, and many of them quite beautiful. Their hair was much finer than that of the men, and they took great pride in it.

Maquina's favorite wife, the mother of Sat-sat

L

was a Wickanninish princess, and a woman whom John thought, would have been called handsome in any country. She was tall and majestic in her figure, of quite a light complexion; her features were finely formed, and her eyes soft and languishing.

The women were much neater in their habits and about their persons than the men; and one way in which their dress differs, which I forgot to mention before, is, that the former had sleeves to their kutsacks, that were large and loose, and reached to the elbows.

The men were very fond of painting their faces and limbs, and they would often spend much time in performing this favorite business of the *toilette.* And, after great patience in laying on the paint, in such colors and figures as they had chosen, if the face thus coated did not happen to suit its possessor, he would wash it all clean, and begin his daubing anew.

The women used very little paint, only drawing a black, curved line over each eyebrow, and a bright red streak from each corner of the mouth, towards the ear; but they were very fond of ornaments, such as ear rings, finger rings, necklaces, bracelets, nose jewels, &c.

Many of these ornaments were made of brass and copper; but the wives of the king and chiefs had their nose jewels and necklaces of a small white shell, that formed a kind of bead, and when strung in rows, it looked very beautiful.

This shell which they called *Ife-maw*, they valued very highly. It was about as large round as a goose quill; and three inches long; of a cylindrical form, a little curved, and tapering gradually to a point at the ends, which were broken off by the natives, so as to admit of its being run on a string. It was of a polished smoothness and white as snow, and formed a very handsome ornament.

The ife-maw formed a sort of money among the natives; and five fathoms of it, strung on threads of bark, was the price of a slave, which they held as very valuable property.

It was brought to Nootka principally, by other tribes, as very little of it could be found there; but it was taken in great abundance, though with much labor and difficulty, from among the reefs of rocks on the coast about forty miles beyond.

The ife-maw fisher went to his work in the following way: A number of sharp pine pegs being fastened in the end of a piece of plank, so as to form a set of teeth, he fastened on the plank, a stone or some other *weighty matter*, so as to carry it down in the water.   Then he fastened the plank to one end of a pole, to the other end of which he tied a line of such a length that he could let it down, or take it up at will.

Provided with this odd sort of a machine the Indian went out in his canoe, skimming round the reefs where he thought the shells grew.

He let down his plank, as if sounding, till it touched the bottom, and then lifting it and letting it fall several times, would at length, bring it up with the shells fastened on the ends of the pegs.

But the ife-maw fisher earned his treasures by much toil, for he would often work a great while to bring up a few shells, as there would frequently come up, not more than two or three at a time.

In addition to painting their faces, sometimes, one half red, and the other black, and sometimes all over in small checks, the men of Nootka had another way of dressing them, that was certainly very showy, to say the least; but the privilege of doing this was not allowed to any but the chiefs.

After spreading the face all over with bear's oil, they strewed it with a fine, black, shining powder, till it quite covered it, and sticking to the oil, sparkled in the sun, and glittered like silver.

When people are insincere, or unequal in their spirits, or behavior, we often hear it figuratively said of them, that they have *two faces*. But these whimsical Indians had, literally, many faces, or rather, many dresses for the face, and they changed them, as capriciously as a fashionable belle will change her ball-dress.

This shining powder, which the Nootkans valued very highly, they called *pelpelth*. It was brought to them in bags, by one of the tribes at the

North, who gathered it among the rocks, and sold it at a high price.

From this tribe which bear the name of *Newche-mass*, they obtained also their finest paints.

Though the natives employed so much paint about their persons, as it was put on with oil, their habit of going into the sea water every day, to bathe, did not injure it much, if any; and whenever they wanted to remove the paint, they would go to a place where there was fresh water, and scrub themselves with sand and rushes.

When going to a festival, or on any great occasion, the Indians spent much time, not only in preparing their faces, but also in dressing the head, which was done in the following way:

The hair, being liberally oiled, was drawn up, smooth and carefully, on the top of the head, and fastened in a tuft, with a large green branch of spruce or pine, with all the leaves on, confined in it, and touched with turpentine or gum, so as to make the white down with which it was to be powdered, adhere.

Then, the head and branch were carefully ornamented by a semi-covering of the said white down, which was obtained from the eagles that inhabited the coast in great numbers.

This must have been a fanciful, and somewhat tasteful head-dress; if not as costly as a whole bird of Paradise, worn by a fashionable lady, it was certainly not a more odd or strange imagination for head gear; and if a beautiful, fair face had been beneath it, it might have had quite an effect.

The white down of the eagle, and the fresh, green branch from the forest, seemed to be quite tastefully chosen, and they might have set well above the pretty face of a white lady, who in giving up her bird, with its sweeping trail, to perch upon the head of the Indian, above his painted or shining, plaistered face, would have made no bad exchange, and put things more in keeping.

Or, if a lady would even set out the tree first in her head, and then let the bird light upon it, it would seem more like nature; and nature appears to be the object when one carries an entire fowl about upon the uppermost part of the person, however much art may be employed in placing and displaying the beautiful specimen of the workmanship of its Maker.

The men as well as the women of Nootka, wore bracelets of painted leather and copper, and nose jewels of various materials, and formed in divers shapes; such as hearts, diamonds, &c.

The chiefs, beside the brass and copper ornaments for the nose, had also a bright bluish-colored shell, of a twisted, conical form, and about half an inch long, which they wore suspended by a wire, or a thread, that went through the gristle of the nose, in a hole that, made in infancy for the purpose, was kept open by means of a wooden pin, and enlarged till it became of the size of the pipe stem, in diameter.

The common people, who could not afford to wear a more expensive ornament, had, many of them, smooth sticks of wood, polished for the purpose, which, passing through the perforated place, came out on each side, several inches beyond the face.

Thompson used to call the wearers of these strange ornaments, ' *Sprit-sail-yard fellows ;*' and as he saw one of them coming towards him, with an air of importance which seemed to him proportionate to the length of the stick, he would hold up his hand so that the stick should come violently against it in passing, to the no small discomfort of its wearer's nose. This, he said, he did, ' in order to brace them up a little to the breeze. '

CHAPTER XII.

*Of the religion—the government—certain offices—the disposi-
tion of the natives—their oratory—their diseases, cures, &c.—
the climate.*

BEFORE our narrative is resumed, it may be well
to say something concerning the religion, government, &c. of the people whom it concerns.

John found that the Nootka Indians had a belief
in a Supreme Being, whom they called *Quahootze;*
and who, they said, was one great Tyee, the greatest of all kings.

They said he lived in the sky;—that he gave
them all their fish, and could withhold it or take it
from them when he pleased.

They usually went alone into a retired place in
the woods, or into the water, to worship, and offer
up their prayers. Whenever they bathed, they
addressed a prayer, in a few words, to God, entreating him to preserve their health and to bless their

labors while fishing, to give them success in whaling, war, and other enterprises.

Whenever they were going to war, or a whaling, their prayers always seemed to be offered with more fervor and energy, than at any other time.

When they went into the woods for devotional purposes, they often retired to the distance of a mile or two; and this secrecy, John sometimes suspected, arose from their wish to address God on account of some family or private quarrel, in such a way, or with such requests, as they wanted to keep from all human ears.

He once found a woman in the forest, two miles from the village, kneeling, with her eyes closed and her face turned upward, towards heaven, uttering in a lamentable tone, a prayer, in which she repeated with great fervor, *Wocash Ah-Welth?* (good Lord.) He came close to her, but she seemed wrapped in her devotions, and insensible to every thing around her.

The women frequently retired in this way; and when they returned to the village, their silence and melancholy looks told on what their minds had been employed.

When the Nootkans were going to war with another tribe, they passed much time in the water, where they scrubbed themselves from head to foot, with bushes and briers till they were covered with blood, while all the time they repeated a prayer, that may be translated thus:

'Great God! let me live—not be sick—find the enemy—not fear him—find him asleep, and kill a great many many of him.'

Independent of this scratching ceremony, which was done by way of hardening them for war, the idea of their going into the sea to worship God, had a good deal of beauty and sublimity in it. It was certainly a noble temple that they chose, in this, as well as in the forest, which was also a grand sanctuary with many firm pillars, beautiful curtains, and filled with the sounds of music from the voices of the birds and the sweeping of the winds.

The parents of twin children, the natives considered as being favored with some peculiar notice and with special communication from Quahootze, and their persons were held as too sacred to mingle with others at their festivals, or to do any labor for two years.

During this time, they lived secluded lives, being provided with food by the others; and wearing no ornaments, they kept away from all amusements, and became recluse in everything.

The father wore around his head a red fillet as a sign of solemnity, and always appeared serious and thoughtful. He became a kind of priest, and went daily to the mountain with a chief's rattle in his hand, to pray Quahootze to bring fish into their waters, and to sing and make music to him with the rattle.

He never went out, except on such an errand as this, and to sing and perform religious rites and ceremonies over the sick.

The government of the Nootka Indians was vested in a hereditary king, and descended to his eldest male heir.   But in case of his dying without a son, it went to his brother.

The king had no legal right over the property of his subjects, nor did it appear that he expected them to contribute to his support any more than to that of each other.

But he was the head of their councils, and their leader in war, in the management of which, his power was absolute.

The right of holding slaves was shared between him and the chiefs, but the subject did not possess this privilege.   The slaves were people taken in war, from other tribes, and considered the king's property, which he divided, according to his own judgment, among the chiefs, and with due regard to their rank and merits.

At the age of seventeen, the eldest son of a chief was considered a chief himself; and whenever a father, who was a chief, made a present, it was always done in the name of his eldest son.

The chiefs frequently purchased their wives

when they were not more than eight or nine years old, to prevent their being engaged to others; but they remained with their parents till sixteen, or thereabouts.

Among themselves, the Nootkans seemed pacific and inoffensive, and manifested naturally good tempers. Quarrels seldom occurred between any of them.

But if they happened to get a little offended, they had a way of seeming terribly enraged, which appeared to be rather a matter of fashion than of feeling.

This they did by kicking, spitting, foaming at the mouth, and stamping with great fury.

An exhibition of this sort was made more by custom, and for effect, than for any feelings of malignity; and the same show of conduct was carried on in their assemblages for public speeches, where, he who raved and stamped with the most violence, and went through the greatest variety of contortions, was considered the greatest orator.

The people of Nootka were very healthy, and

seldom had any disease among them, but the cholic, which they commonly cured by rubbing the bowels of the patient, till the pain was allayed.

They cured the rheumatism by scarifying the part affected; and their only remedy for a wound was, to wash it in salt water, and bind it up with a piece of bark, or cloth.

They were very skilful in the management of dislocated or fractured limbs, and when they were set and properly dressed, they took great care to have them supported by blocks, in a right position, and they had generally perfect success in performing the cure.

In cases of sickness, while those who performed the office of physician and nurse, were busy in their respective ways, the holy man, or conjuror, was employed in going through certain strange gestures, repeating his words of wisdom, singing and blowing, to blow off the evil spirit. If it was a case of cholic, the patient, after going through the rubbing, was wrapped in a bear skin, to produce perspiration.

With such treatment the sick generally recovered, and a death among them, where the population was about fifteen hundred, was a thing of rare occurrence. The natives commonly lived to be very old.

The climate at Nootka, and the neighboring region, was found by our adventurers, to be very mild. The spring, summer and autumn were uncommonly delightful; and the winter, which did not set in till the last of December, was short, and not at all severe. Water seldom froze to a depth of more than three inches, and the snow, in its greatest fall, was not more than four inches deep.

But what did not fall in snow, did in rain; for it frequently rained during the winter months, five or six days in succession.

CHAPTER XIII.

Population of Nootka—making of canoes—pursuit of sea-otters —description of one—the Indian's fish-hook and fishing— Maquina's household—instruments of music.

I HAVE stated that the inhabitants of Nootka were about fifteen hundred, and the buildings were about twenty in number.

But, besides the Nootka tribe, there was a small tribe whom they had conquered and made subject to them, and who inhabited a cluster of small houses, that stood near the other twenty of the village.

This tribe was called *Klahars.* They lived by themselves, but had no chiefs of their own, being wholly under Maquina's government.

I dare say, my young reader, that you are now growing impatient to have me resume the thread of my story, and that you think I have made a very long digression from it.

And so I have, but it has enabled you to understand the better, what sort of a place John was in, what kind of people he was among, and how many odd ways and whims he had to conform to, in his new condition, where he had literally 'new lords and new laws.'

You can now imagine just how one of the Indians looked when dressed for an excursion, or decked out for a feast.

You now want to be told how they made their canoes; for they were things of so much importance that we shall often make mention of them.

The first step towards this work, was to fell a tree, by working round it with the chisel, which was a very slow and laborious business, especially when they wanted a canoe of the largest kind, for they made them of all sizes, from that which would contain only one man, up to one that would hold forty.

The largest were the war canoes.   It took three

Indians about a day, to fell a tree, which being done, they took of the trunk, the length they wanted, and then dug it out with their chisels inside, and fashioned it to their minds on the outside.

They then put light combustibles round, and in it, and made a blaze, which took off all the loose splinters, and left it quite black. The next step was to rub it hard all over, with a piece of matting, till it became quite smooth and polished.

The inside was then painted red, with red ochre, and the figure of a bird, such as a duck or some other water-fowl formed of separate pieces of wood and painted, and then divided and fastened on, the head part on the prow, and the tail, on the stern of the canoe.

The war-canoes were painted on the outside, with white chalk, in figures representing men's heads, moons, eagles, whales, &c.

The others were ornamented with double rows of white shells, that formed a kind of bead-work all round them, and had a very pretty effect as they were skimming along over the surface of the waters, looking like things half bird, half fish.

The Indians used the paddle with great dexterity, and gliding swiftly over the waves, kept time to its stroke by some wild musical strains. They always had a song for every occasion, which varied according to the nature of the business of the excursion.

John used frequently to go out with them in these light skimmers of the sea; and we will now imagine him with a company of natives dressed as they have been described, and topped off with their sugar-loaf caps, going out in pursuit of the sea-otter.

This animal was to John a very beautiful sight as it sported round the canoes, and would dive suddenly under water, and come out some where at a distance, as if playing at bo-peep.

He found the length of the otter to be about six feet from the head to the tip of the tail. It was of a beautiful glossy black all over except a white stripe on the top of the head and a little tip of it on the end of the tail, which tapered off to a point; but it was thick and bushy near the body.

As the otter swam along, with its head entirely above water, having between its sharp, upright ears a tuft of long hair that stood erect, and made its head look as if it had three short horns, John thought he had never seen a more beautiful object.

The skin of this creature was considered very valuable by the natives. The young sea-otters were so exceedingly small, that when John first saw them he was puzzled to make out what they could be.

A troop of them came swimming beside or round the old one, and were not larger than rats, and our hero, after some time, discovered it to be a mother with her family of baby otters, that followed her through the waves as the chickens follow the hen over the field.

The fish-hook used by the natives when John went among them, was formed by a sharp-bearded piece of bone inserted in a piece of wood, and bound in by a string of whale-sinew; but when they found how much faster they could take the fish with the iron hooks that he made, they were, for once, willing to give up their own old way, and use the new-fashioned hook.

_ In fishing for salmon, they baited the hook with a sprat, and fastening the line to the end of the paddle with which they sped their canoe, let it down, and kept it in motion as if alive, under the water, till the salmon snapped at it and was caught by the hook.

In taking the whale they were very dexterous. To kill him, they struck at him with a kind of javelin or harpoon of their own invention, and made of wood, bone, shell, and whale sinew.

The whale was considered by them as the royal mark, and no person, however near he might be, was permitted to strike at him, till the king's harpoon had first drawn blood. It was held as a sacrilegious deed for a common person to strike the king's fish before his majesty and the chiefs had killed him.

I do not know exactly how large a number of

people comprised the family in which our friends John and Thompson had to live; but the slaves alone, of Maquina's household, were about fifty, including male and female, some of which were purchased from other tribes, and some were taken in war.

I have alluded to the music of the Nootkans, but not particularly. Their tunes were soft and plaintive, and very harmonious.

When they sang, their voices were accompanied by some rude kind of instrument. Their drum, I think, I have described. The noise it made was similar to that of the empty cask when the head is drummed on, and very loud.

The rattle and pipe, or whistle, were the king's instruments, and only used by him and the chiefs, or some honorable personage.

The rattle was formed of a piece of seal-skin, in the shape of a fish, and painted red. The inside contained small pebbles enough to make the music, and it had a handle by which it was held and shaken.

I suspect it was as noisy a fish as ever had a being, and that it was longer in motion than any other ' fish out of water.'

The whistle was made of a short piece of the leg-bone of a deer; and sent forth a sprightly, shrill sound. Thus, a part of the animal's leg kept *going*, when the rest of him had long been, as the chemist would say, 'decomposed;' and, like the farmer's boy that the poet describes, it ' whistled as it went, for want of thought.'

The Nootkans were, on the whole, a queer set of people; and they might truly be said to have ' sought out many inventions,' though some of these were not the wisest in the world.

Another sort of instrument that they used, was a sort of castanet, formed of cockle-shells, tied together and shaken to a tune which the musician sung.

This, I think, was quite a pretty fancy; and I suspect it originated in the head of some poetical savage.

CHAPTER XIV.

Different tribes of natives—some of their customs—dressing for a visit—manner of making a bargain—lodging of the visiters—their arms.

So many different tribes of natives came to visit those of Nootka, that our captives had an opportunity of observing a great variety of manners and looks, some of which were disgusting, some terrific, and others very amusing.

The *Wickanninish* was the tribe to which *Y-ya-tinkla-no*, the mother of Sat-sat, and Maquina's favorite *Arcomah*, or queen, belonged. She was the daughter of their king.

They lived at the north, about two hundred miles from Nootka, and had among them, from six to seven hundred warriors. In their persons, they were robust, and in their spirit, very courageous. They had broad faces, but heads that, from their manner of pressing and binding them when young, rose high, somewhat in the sugar-loaf form. They often visited Nootka, and a close friendship subsisted between the two nations.

The *Kla-iz-zarts* belonged about three hundred miles to the south, and were a numerous and powerful tribe, having nearly a thousand warriors.

They were more neatly dressed, were more pleasing and mild in their manners, and appeared more civilized than any other tribe. They were sprightly, and affable, and much celebrated for their singing and dancing.

Their canoes were more finely finished and ornamented, and all their workmanship manifested greater skill than appeared in any other tribe.

Their complexions were fairer than those of Nootka, their noses not so prominent, and their eyes smaller. Their heads were flattened on the top, as if pressed by a weight; and their stature was rather shorter than that of the Nootkans.

They had one practice not followed by any

other tribe; it was that of plucking out, not only their beards, but their eyebrows also, so as not to leave a sign of it remaining.

They manifested more taste and skill, than any others, in decorating and painting their persons, and some of them would have a dozen holes in their ears, through which they passed little strings of beads about two inches long, and of various colors.

These people were great whalers, and very expert in taking the sea-otter, the metamelth, and the beaver. Of the hair of the latter, and that of the tiger-cat, they manufactured a handsome kind of gray cloth.

The *Eskquates* were a tribe about as large as the Wickanninish, and were tributary to Maquina.

The *Aitizzarts* were a smaller tribe, who were also tributary to Nootka, and greatly resembled its inhabitants in their appearance and practices. They lived about forty miles up the sound.

Farther to the northward were the *Cayuquets*, a more numerous tribe than the Nootkans, by whom they were considered such bad warriors, and so deficient in courage, that they said they had little hearts, like those of birds.

John saw a great many tribes of which I shall not make particular mention; but of all that he saw, the most ugly and frightful looking, were the *Newchemass*, who lived at a great distance inland.

Their complexions were darker, their hair coarser, and their stature shorter than those of any others; and they were extremely squalid about their persons.

Their beards grew long like a Jew's: their dress was a kutsack of wolf skin, with tails hanging from top to bottom of the garment. Sometimes, they wore a mantle of cloth. Their hair was left to hang down loose behind; but that on the other parts of the head was brought round the forehead like a fillet, and confined by a strip of cloth, ornamented with rows of shells.

Their weapons were the *Cheetoolth*, or war club,

formed of whale bone, daggers, and bows and arrows, and a bone or copper spear.

The merchandise they brought to trade with, was the shining black mineral which 1 have spoken of by the name of pelpelth, which sparkled on the Indian faces; some wolf skins, dried salmon, the roe of fish, red paint, clams, and a coarse matting.

As they had to come a great distance, and a part of it by land, they used to make longer visits at Nootka, than any other tribe, in order to recover from their fatigue. On these occasions, they joined in the amusements and taught their own songs, &c. to the Nootkians.

The things which other tribes brought for sale, or for presents, were principally train-oil, whale or seal blubber, fish of various kinds, clams, muscles, a kind of fruit called *yama*, that was pressed and dried, cloth, otter skins and slaves.

They also brought the Ife-maw, wild ducks, and a very pleasant kind of root, called *Quanoose*. This root seemed to take the place of the potato.

It was pear-shaped, and about as large as a small onion. It was brought in baskets, all ready cooked by steam, and fit for eating, and was sweet, mealy, and pleasant to the taste.

But the depraved taste of the natives would not be satisfied, even with this delicious root, without the dressing of train-oil to make it go down well.

Many of these things were offered to Maquina as tributary gifts in token of his superiority; but the cunning ones who brought them usually took good care to get full their worth, and sometimes more, in presents from the king and his people.

When a company of visitors came, there was always a great feast made for them, and tub after tub was filled with blubber, roe, salmon, &c. of which all the men, women and children of the village were invited to partake.

As they had no intoxicating liquors, and knew no way of making any, their intemperance on these occasions was shown by inordinate eating, their drink being only water.

The visitors, when they got within a few miles

of the village, used to stop under the lee of some high rock, and attend to the *toilette*. Here they dressed themselves for the party, in all their best attire, and put on their best faces, by painting, oiling, powdering, &c.

They did as many others do, when going to a party; they put on all their ornaments, took great pains to dress their heads, and to make a dazzling appearance; an attempt not always confined to those only, who are going to the king's festival.

On arriving at the shore, they were met by the king, who first invited them to eat; when they brought him such goods as they supposed he wished to receive. After this, other natives were allowed to purchase, the strangers taking good care to keep their merchandise under guard in their canoes, till sold, to avoid their being stolen by the *light-fingers* among the natives, who considered pilfering no sin if it was not discovered.

But when some particular purchase was the object of the new comer, he would keep his canoe a

little off from the shore, and send forward an am-
bassador, tricked out in his best, and with his
head touched off with the white down, to stand
in the prow and display his goods, making known
the purpose of their owner and the price that he
was willing to give in such articles as were shown,
for the purchase he wished to make.

If the bargain was agreed on, the exchange was
made at once.

On visits either of friendship or trade, none of
the strangers, except the kings and chiefs, were
allowed to sleep on shore; and they lodged at the
king's house. The others passed the night in their
canoes. This was partly for the preservation of
their own goods from the inhabitants, and partly
an arrangement of theirs, to prevent danger to
themselves and their property from their crafty and
thievish visitors.

These people were always armed; the com-
moners, with a dagger, slung at the neck, and
hanging behind by a strip of metamelth, and sometimes with a bow and arrows; but the latter had

almost grown out of use, in consequence of the introduction of fire arms among them.

The chiefs, in addition to the dagger, wore the cheetoolth, or war club, of which I have spoken. This weapon, made of the bone of a whale, with a blade eighteen inches long, three broad, and very heavy, was a powerful thing in the hand of a strong man. The blade was thick in the middle, but thinned off to an edge on each side, and expanded in width towards the end, to increase the force of the blow.

It was covered with figures, such as, the sun, moon, men's heads, and other devices of curious inventions; and the hilt wrought in the form of a human head, was fancifully inlaid with shells, and had a strip of metamelth fastened to it, by which to sling it over the shoulder.

They had, also, a sort of spear, headed with copper, or the bone of the sting-ray, which was a weapon of great destruction when wielded by one of a firm hand and bold spirit.

CHAPTER XV.

Place of retirement for worship—its scenery,—the Sabbath—a ship seen—a thunder storm—hard fare—arts of other natives —a young girl tries to win John—the Nootkans remove to winter quarters—the place.

DURING all this exhibition of new faces, new modes, and new things, John and his companion fared better than they could have expected at the beginning of their sorrows.

But day after day did their longing eyes stretch out their sight in vain over the great waters, to catch a glimpse of some sail that might give them a gleaming hope of deliverance.

About a mile from the village there was a beautiful fresh-water pond, of a quarter of a mile in breadth, and surrounded by a forest of evergreen trees. The pond was smooth and clear as crystal, and the forest free of all annoyance from under-wood or bramble.

It was filled with the music of a thousand birds, and beautiful with their gay and diversified plumage. The bright little humming-birds came to it, as a favorite resort; and they were seen hovering round the low flowers, or pen'ing from the green boughs, like jewels kept in motion by some power of the airy element.

This pond was seldom visited by the natives, except for the purpose of taking off a coat of paint. It furnished, therefore, a calm and delightful retreat to our captives, who used to retire to it every Sunday, and after bathing freely in its waters, and exchanging their garments for the clean ones that they had before washed in it, and left on its margin to dry, they spent the rest of the day in devotion to Him, whom it was their chief consolation to find was the God of the wilderness, as well as of the garden and the city.

They took their Bible and Prayer Book with them, and, seated under a noble, umbrageous pine,

John read aloud, while Thompson listened, and the feathered multitude performed the part of choir, in singing praises to their Maker.

This scene of worship and supplication, in such a solitude, presents a sublime and beautiful picture to the imagination. The speaker and his single auditor just made up one of the numbers to whom our Savior has promised his presence and his blessing, when they meet together in his name.

And here in this lonely wild, trodden only by the feet of the savage, and the beast of the forest were these unfortunate men thrown, to learn, in the bosom of nature, the value of the Bible and the consolations of the Christian religion.

John felt the parting advice of his good father written on his heart; and the promises of Him, who used to go himself into the forest, and on the mountains, to pray, were kept in his bosom, whispering peace to his soul, amid all the horrors of captivity, and the hopelessness of the outward circumstances that surrounded him.

God, who declares that the hearts of kings are in

JEWETT AND THOMPSON KEEPING THE SABBATH.

his hands, here showed, that civilized royalty was not alone comprehended in the declaration. His power was manifested on the heart of the red monarch of the wood. Maquina, when he learnt that the purpose for which his prisoners retired on the Sabbath was to worship their God, felt too great a reverence for the object to have their devotions interrupted, or to forbid them the privilege of going by themselves, for the purpose of communing with the great Being whom they adored.

Some time in July, hope suddenly flashed into the heart of John and his new father, from a distant sail that appeared for a few minutes; but it passed on without coming near the land, and all was gloom again, as it respected the prospect of seeing a Christian face.

A few days after this, there came up a violent thunder storm. The people of the village all fled from their own houses, and hurried to that of their king, where, instead of going within for shelter, they got on the roof of the house, seating themselves as thick as they could, and have room to drum.

The king commenced drumming and singing, and looking up to the sky, and all the people joined in, making a most tremendous noise with their sticks on the boards, and their loud vociferations, while they entreated Quahootze not to kill them.

This religious ceremony, expressive of fear and supplication, was kept up till the storm had subsided.

Things went on in rather a monotonous manner, till towards the decline of summer, when the king and his men, going out for whaling on the coast, left the prisoners at home, for fear that they might escape to some other tribe on the coast, if permitted to go with them.

Meantime, as the women seldom cooked much when the king and the men were gone, the prisoners often found themselves brought to a scanty fare, and felt the cravings of hunger.

Sometimes they were fortunate enough to procure a good piece of salmon, which they would boil in salt water, with a few nettles for greens, and some scattering turnips and onions, which they gleaned from the remains of the Spanish garden, and with these, in secret, make up quite a comfortable meal.

They often heard from the tribes of the north and south, who came to Nootka, stories of vessels that were seen coming to land, along their coast, and were advised to go with them, with the promise that they would protect and see them safe on board one that might carry them to their country.

But these accounts they found were all false, and only a lure held out by these crafty savages, to get them out of Maquina's hands into their own, for slaves. Yet, preferring to remain with present evils, to going where their situation might be rendered worse, they turned a deaf ear to these persuasions.

Among other inducements offered to John, to make his escape from Nootka, a young lady of the forest took it into her head to fall greatly in love with him; and this young lady was a princess too, belonging to a powerful tribe.

She was a daughter of the Wickanninish king, and younger sister of Maquina's queen. She was a beautiful Indian girl, quite fair, and of fine features; but she had received an injury in one of her eyes, that had impaired the sight. This, Maquina told John, would forever prevent her being married; as a defect of this kind was an insuperable objection to a female, in the view of an Indian who was choosing a wife.

But the young one-eyed beauty thought she would outwit the fastidious beaux of her own color, by securing to herself a white companion.

She therefore flattered and coaxed John to go with her to her father's people, telling him he would there have better food and clothing, and kinder treatment; and that if he wished it, they would put him into a vessel and let him go home.

She asked him about his friends, in his own country; and if he had not a mother and sister who would mourn for him till he returned.

But, as John had no idea of ingrafting himself as a branch into the royal family of the wood, he

decidedly declined all the splendor of such an alli-
ance, and rejected the offer with the firmness of a
true philosopher; and the Wickanninish fair was
left to bemoan her disappointed hopes. The name
of this princess was Yuqua.

Early in September, the Nootkans made preparations to depart from this, their summer residence,
to plant themselves for the autumn and winter on
a less exposed and more agreeable spot, according
to their usual custom; their village being located
where the winds were cold, and brought the storms
from the sea in upon them.

The places to which they resorted at these seasons, were Tashees and Cooptee. The latter place
was about thirty miles up the sound, and lay in a
deep bay; but it was very difficult of access by
canoes, on account of the reefs of dangerous rock
that lay in the way.

Tashees was not far from it, and situated in a
small hollow at the foot of a mountain, on the south
shore.

This place afforded a beautiful view of romantic

scenery, that was very pleasant to the eye; and the noise of the rivulets and cascades, that rippled and sparkled on the sides of the mountains, addressed the ear with a native and inimitable music.

The spot on which the town stood, with its houses in a string like these of Nootka, was level, the soil good; and a noble river, about twenty rods vide, rolled by it.

The buildings here were not so large as those at Vootka, and the people had to accommodate each other as well as they could by stowing closely together. One great object in the choice of this spot, was the facility it afforded the natives for procuring their winter provisions.

A lofty range of high hills ran along on each side of Tashees, covered with beautiful forest trees, and extending inland to a great distance.

CHAPTER XVI.

The scene of departure—conveyance of their infants—an anecdote of St. John's Indians—passage to Tashees—arrival and business there—manner of taking roe fish, &c.—how they were cured and cooked—John's condition.

THE time of preparation for leaving Nootka presented a busy, bustling scene, and one that would have greatly amused the captives, had they beheld it for the first time, under happier circumstances than now attended them.

If it was not, literally, plucking up stakes, it was plucking off boards; for, even the coverings of their houses were stripped away, to load the canoes, and be carried with them, to lay on the roofs and inclose the sides of the habitations they were going to occupy.

Thus, they removed and changed the outside of their buildings as they did their own garments, to suit their convenience, leaving only the posts standing in the place they were about to desert till they returned to it in another season.

Boxes, baskets, tubs, men, women and pappooses were all huddled together into the canoes and the long-boat of the ship, which, having been repaired and furnished with a sail by Thompson, was loaded as deep as she could swim, and put under the management of the prisoners, the natives finding themselves rather green hands at steering the boat.

Having got all their worldly goods afloat, they pushed off from shore, turning their backs on the naked posts of their town, that stood looking like desolation.

The infant children, for transportation in a removal of this sort, were laid into little bark cradles, or hammocks, about six inches deep, and just long and wide enough to contain them. They were then laced in, by a string passing through the edges of their vehicle, and slung at the backs of their mothers.

I believe it is a general practice among all our

Indians, to lace their young infants flat upon their backs, in a straight position, to a piece of board or in a cradle of this sort, in order to have their forms erect, when they grow up. This is thought to be the reason why the savages are generally so well shaped and erect.

I once saw, among a company of St. John's Indians, an infant only a few days old, laced down in this way to a small piece of board, as closely as a little fish, pegged down to dry.

I went with several friends to visit the encampment, which was in an extensive cleared ground, about an eighth of a mile from the road. As we left our carriages by the road-side to enter the field, we perceived near the wall, a little savage about four years old, who had strayed away from the wigwams, and was peeping at us through the crevices between the stones.

One of our company smacked his whip suddenly at him to startle him; at which he was so affrighted, that he took to his little red heels, and went full speed, and screaming, to the wigwams; and we lost sight of him among the others at the encampment, which we did not reach till some time after he had got safe home.

The Indians treated us very civilly, as we went round from one habitation to another; showing us their basket-stuff, &c. and letting us creep, one at a time, as well as we could, into their huts, that were made of bark, and resembled a thicket of haycocks, more than anything else, when viewed at a distance.

We were asked if we did not want to see a little infant that was in one of these huts, which we had not entered, and told that we might see it laced to its board, for six cents apiece.

So we drew near the entrance, throwing in our toll one at a time, when the mother, after she had made sure of the fee, would lift the blanket that was thrown over the child, and give the spectator one peep, and then let it fall.

The gentleman who had smacked the whip, but who had entirely forgotten the act, and myself, happened to be the two last.

He threw in a nine-penny piece, saying that was for both of us. The mother took the money, and beckoned to me to come first. When I had had my peep, and passed out, the gentleman went forward for his.

But the cunning and handsome young mother shrouded her child in another fold of the blanket, and throwing her arms over to hide it, looked up, and with an arch smile, said, '*No, no,—you scare my little boy—you no see—no, no!*'—and with an expression of playful triumph and satisfaction, at having so soon avenged herself for the rudeness offered to her boy, she hugged her baby tight till the disappointed spectator went away.

The child was folded in a little blanket, over which the lacing passed. It is the custom of these Indian mothers, when they are out in the forests, to hang their little bark cradles, with their infants confined in them, on the boughs of trees, for the birds to sing their lullaby, and the breezes to rock them to sleep.

We will now return to our fleet of canoes, and

imagine them, as they went, with all the wealth of Nootka piled up within their sides; while the loud songs of the people poured over the waters and rang along the shore amid the rocks and the trees, as they glided up the sound towards Cooptee, and then passed it, on the way to Tashees.

On arriving at this place, the first business of the people was, to set about covering the skeletons of their houses that were found standing to receive their coat of boards, and to be repeopled by their former lords and masters.

Their habitations prepared, their next work was to provide for themselves the creature comforts that were to be brought up from under the waters, in the form of herring roe, salmon, and other kinds of fish.

In order to take the roe of the herring, which, one would suppose, would be no easy thing to effect, they laid a very curious and successful plan.

They cut immense quantities of broad pine branches, and sunk them where the water was about ten feet deep, fastening them to the bottom by means of heavy stones, that kept them down, till the herring swam up and deposited their roe upon them.

The branches were then taken up, and the roe stripped off by the women, who washed it and cleared it from the pine leaves, and then dried it and put up in baskets for future use.

To take salmon and other fish at this place, they wove a sort of a trap or ware, with flexile twigs; the form of which was somewhat like a pot, or bee-hive.

Its mouth was made by turning the sharpened ends of the twigs in, after the manner of a wire mouse-trap, and sloping to quite a narrow passage, so as to let the fish slip in; and then to cry (*if he could*,) like Sterne's starling, 'I can't get out!'

The prisoners in these water-cages were obliged to come out at length, as the proverb would say, 'at the little end of the horn;' for at the end where the ware tapered off to a point, a place, like a sort of door, was made so as to be opened for remov-

ing the finny dupe, and then closed for the purpose
of entrapping another.

These fish-traps were set immediately below
some rapid, above which the natives went with
their canoes, and drove the fish down, till, fleeing
from one evil, they slipped, unsuspectingly, into
another, and went to sure destruction.

John saw more than seven hundred salmon taken
by this method in the course of fifteen minutes.
Some bass were taken in the same way.

The cod and halibut were cut up into small
pieces, and dried in the sun, for preservation; but
the salmon that was to be cured for winter food,
was split open, the head and back bone were removed, and then it was hung up in the house to
dry.

This season was a time of great feasting and
hilarity among the Indians. They cooked immense quantities of fish, and lived not upon the fat
of the land, but of the waters.

They cooked at Maquina's house, one hundred
salmon at once, in a tub of enormous size, and ate

with the appetite of a people who were not accustomed to make two bites at a cherry.

Tashees was at this time a place of great business, and all hands were engaged, either in catching, curing, or cooking fish, or in conveying it to the mouths of the feasters.

John used frequently to go out with Maquina after salmon; and the king would always allow him a part, to be considered as his share of the spoil.

He used, also, to shoot wild ducks and teal, which the women skinned, and boiled them in the same way that they did their other food.

The prisoners found their condition at this place less comfortable than at Nootka, in some respects, as the weather began to grow cold, and they were obliged to be more within doors; and the houses being smaller, did not accommodate them so well as those they had before occupied.

But they did not neglect to go off alone on the Sabbath to bathe in some stream, and to pass the rest of the day in retirement, by its side, offer-

ing up supplications to God for their deliverance,
and thanks for the preservation of their lives, until
the winter came on so cold as to cut them short of
this privilege, by obliging them to stay near a
shelter and a fire.

CHAPTER XVII.

John forbidden to write—a new dress made for the king—he accounts for having killed the crew—the yama—taking the bear—singular ceremony—an annual thanksgiving.

JOHN had not been long at Tashees, when he began to feel serious alarm for the fate of his journal. Maquina, who saw him writing in it from day to day, told him that if he saw him engaged at it again, he would certainly destroy it.

John told him he was keeping accounts of the weather; but the sagacious king said he knew better, and that he was speaking bad about him and his people for destroying the crew, so as to inform his countrymen against them, if he could meet with any who came upon the coast. After this, John had to be very secret about his writing.

He finished about this time, some highly-polish

ed daggers, and made a cheetoolth after the king's directions, that pleased his majesty highly.

Thompson began to grow into the king's favor, also, for having made a fine sail for his canoe, and a kutsack for him by stitching European vest patterns together till he formed a mantle a fathom square.

This garment, comprised of various pieces and figures, and variegated with all the colors of the rainbow, must certainly have exceeded Joseph's coat, in its ornaments, if not in the many hues it exhibited; for to finish it off in style, Thompson had put on its edge a border of otter-skin, and above this, six rows of gilt buttons, as thick as they could be set together.

The arm-holes were bordered in the same way and the king put it on, and strutted about with all the pride of a peacock, while the buttons tinkled as he went, and his people looked at him as at a shining idol.

He rewarded Thompson for his skill, and gave John a piece of European cloth large enough to make him a good suit of clothes for the winter, as a token of gratification for his having finished the daggers and the cheetoolth so well.

Not long after this, he showed John a book in which were seven names of persons who had belonged to the ship Manchester of Philadelphia, commanded by Captain Brian. These were Daniel Smith, Louis Gillon, James Tom, Clark, Ben, Johnson, and Jack.

These men, Maquina said, deserted the ship and came to him; and that six of them ran away afterwards, in order to go to the Wickanninish. But being stopped on the way by another tribe, they were sent back to him, and put to a cruel death.

One of the natives told John that the way in which these men were killed was this:—Four Indians took a man at a time, and held him down, while others crowded stones down his throat: thus one after the other was despatched.

Jack, the boy who did not attempt to escape, was sold to the Wickanninish king; but, according to the account of Yuqua, the princess, he had to work so hard that his health failed; and when he heard of the murder of his friends, it affected him so much, that he fell sick and died.

Maquina, finding that John had a great desire to learn their language, took much pleasure in conversing and in trying to teach him.   In one of his conversations, he fully explained the cause of his having destroyed the crew of the Boston.

He said he bore no ill-will towards white men in general; but that he had been several times so badly treated by them, that he had resolved on revenge for the injury they had done him, in repeated instances.

He said the first outrage was committed by a Captain Tawnington, who had passed the winter with his vessel at Friendly Cove, and received kind treatment from the natives.

But when he was gone for his wife, to the Wickanninish, the captain and his men had entered their houses in the absence of the men, terrified the women, and robbed their boxes of all that was valuable.

He said they stole from his store no less than forty fine skins, and made off with their booty.

The next grievance was from a Spanish captain, who barbarously murdered four of the natives. The third was very soon after, from a captain Hanna, of the Sea-Otter, who, because one of the natives stole a chisel from the carpenter, fired upon them, and killed more than twenty, among whom were several Tyees.

Maquina said he was himself on board the vessel at the time, and came near being killed, saving his life only, by leaping from the quarter-deck, and swimming a great distance with his head under water.

He said he had, from that time, determined to avenge the blood of his people, when a fair opportunity presented itself; and that, when Captain Salter insulted him, the feeling of injury and the desire of revenge were roused in his bosom, and he resolved to wait no longer for vengeance on the race of men who had wronged him and slain his brethren.

This tale revealed some sad secrets respecting the conduct of those who had been at Nootka for trade, and received kind treatment from the natives; and it is much to be lamented that civilized men, and those who took the name of Christians, should not have acted more according to the rules of justice and humanity.

One kind of provision which the natives made it serious business to lay in for the winter, while at Tashees, was the *Yama*, a kind of fruit that grew in the woods in great profusion; and which the women went out in companies to gather, with guards of men to protect them from wild beasts.

A yama party would stay several days at a time, in the forest, making for themselves a covert of leafy boughs for the night, and busying themselves during the day in filling their baskets with fruit.

This fruit was a berry, that grew in clusters, upon bushes about three feet high, with large, round and polished leaves.   The berry was black, of an oblong round, and about as large as grapeshot. Its taste was sweet, with a little flavor of acid.

The women would sometimes bring in a dozen bushels of these berries at once, and spread them on blankets: they then laid others over them, to press them, and left them to dry till they were fit to put up in baskets.

Though fish and fruit were the main articles of food among these people, they sometimes used to eat the flesh of the bear, deer, and other animals.

But they had an odd superstition that obliged them, whenever they had eaten of the bear, to abstain from eating fish for two months afterwards; for they believed that, if they ate fish immediately after having fed on the bear, the fish would know it all around, and be so offended as not to come within their waters or suffer themselves to be taken.

Most of the natives were, therefore, unwilling to suffer the penalty of indulging the appetite by a taste of this animal; and when one was taken and dressed, scarcely a dozen of the tribe could be induced to eat of it.

To take the bear, they constructed a trap by the side of some stream, where his black and shaggy honor was in the habit of promenading. This trap was built with post and planks, one of which was so placed, as to let down a heavy load of stones that were laid upon it, when the animal pulled upon a salmon that was suspended to it, by way of bait, within the trap. The head of the beast was, by this means, either crushed, or so forcibly struck as to cause his death at once.

A trap, formed in this manner, was covered with sods, so as to have the appearance of a mound of earth.

Dressing the bear, as the natives called a strange ceremony which they went through, soon after they were established at Tashees, was to John and his companion a very amusing farce, the cause of which was never explained to them.

The animal was taken dead from the trap, cleansed of all the blood and dirt that had ga- thered on him in his hour of distress, and then car- ried to the king's house.

TAKING THE BEAR.

Here, a chief's cap was put upon his head, his body powdered all over with white down, which, contrasted with his black fur, made quite a show. He was then set, in an upright position, opposite the king, and a tray of food put before him, when the Indians urged him, by a variety of words and gestures, to eat.

But Sir Bruin, not showing much inclination to accept the invitations, was soon taken away, skinned, cut up and boiled.

This ceremony was an occasion of great merry-making throughout the village. The king made a great entertainment, and all the people flocked together at the festival, which was generally concluded with a dance by Sat-sat, performed in the way I have already described.

On the morning of December 13th, another strange ceremony began, by the king's firing a pistol, apparently, without a moment's warning, close to the ear of Sat-sat, who dropped down instantly, as if shot dead upon the spot.

Upon this, all the women set up a most terrible

yelling, tearing out their hair by handfuls, and crying out that the prince was dead; when the men rushed in, armed with guns and daggers, inquiring into the cause of the alarm, followed by two of the natives covered with wolf-skins, with masks representing the wolf's head.

These two came in on all-fours, and taking up the prince on their back, carried him out, retiring as they had entered.

Maquina then came to John and Thompson, with a supply of provisions, that he said they must take, and depart with it into the woods, and there remain six days, assuring them that if they return-ed before that time had expired, he should have them killed.

The liberty of going out by themselves for a week would, at a milder season of the year, have been a matter of rejoicing to them; but as it was, they obeyed without delay, and taking their pro-visions, retired into the forest, among the hills and dells, where they passed the time reading, rambling about, &c. during the day time; and at night, they crept under a little covert of boughs woven and made into a small cabin, where they laid themselves down on a bed of leaves, and spread over them the garments that they had taken thither in a bundle, to keep off the cold night air.

On the seventh day after their banishment, they returned to the village, where they found the king, chiefs, and many of the people of another tribe, who had been invited by Maquina to come and keep the week with him, and join in the ceremonies.

It was afterwards ascertained that this grand celebration was an annual thanksgiving, held in honor of Quahootze, to thank him for the favors he had bestowed on them during the year that had elapsed, and to invoke his smile on them for the one now to come.

CHAPTER XVIII.

*Conclusion of the thanksgiving—Christmas kept by the captives—
removal to Cooptee—visit to the Aitizzarts—feast at Cooptee—
false stories of ships—return to Nootka—death of a boy—
insanity of a chief.*

WHAT happened at the village while they were
absent, the prisoners never knew; but the celebration did not end till after their return, and then it
terminated with a shocking and distressing show
of deliberate self-torment.

Three men, each with two bayonets run through
their sides, between the ribs, walked up and down
in the room, singing war-songs, and exulting in
their firmness and triumph over pain.

When the 25th of the month came round, bringing with it a sad sense of the contrast between the
way in which it was celebrated in their native
land, and that in which it must be kept by them,

the captives requested to have the day to themselves, and retiring into the woods, they passed it in reading and other religious exercises, singing the Hymn of the Nativity, and returning thanks for the birth of the Savior.

In the evening, wishing to conform to the customs of good old England, as far as circumstances would permit, they set themselves about getting a better meal than usual, for their *Christmas supper.*

They bought some of the best dainties among the natives, such as, dried clams, &c. and a root which they called *keltsup*, which being cooked by steam, was a very pleasant kind of food; and having made ready their repast, they sat down to make the best of their condition over it, and partook of it with truly grateful hearts, that life, health, and even this homely meal was granted to them in this inhospitable wild.

On the last day of the month, the tribe removed to Cooptee, about fifteen miles from Tashees, which, though not so pleasant as that place, on some accounts, was, from its being nearer to Nootka, beyond which no vessel could come, a more agreeable situation to the prisoners, as they hoped it would allow them a better opportunity of hearing of people of their own nation arriving on the coast.

The first business of the natives at Cooptee, was to cover their houses with their portable roofs and sides.

The next day, January 1st, 1804, the first fall of snow for that winter, came.

About a week afterwards, Maquina took John in his canoe to visit the king of the Aitizzarts, who, with his chiefs, had been to keep the thanksgiving at Tashees, and who had invited Maquina to come to see him at this time, to attend a similar celebration.

This king, whose name was *Upquesta*, had his town about twenty miles from Cooptee, up the sound, and in an extensive valley, on the bank of a noble river.

During the sail to this place, Maquina had told John not to speak, after their arrival, till he made a sign to him.

When they arrived, the king's messenger, who was master of the ceremonies, came out to meet them, dressed in his best, with his head bestrewed with down, and holding in his hand a cheetoolth, the badge of his office.

He saluted them, and conducted them to the presence of the king, with due gravity, pointing out to each, the seat that it belonged to him to take.

Visitors, on these occasions, wore their caps, and took them off as they entered the house. Maquina as he entered, not only doffed his cap, but threw off some of his outer garments, of which he had put on several, one over another.

But very few of the people at this place, who I should have before remarked, welcomed the visitors with loud shouts and the firing of guns, had ever seen a white man, or a European dress; and John was to them an object of no small curiosity.

They flocked about him, feeling of his clothes, his hands, his head, and face, and patting him on the arms and shoulders, as if he had been some animal they had caught, and were glad to find so tame.

As he obeyed the injunction of silence all the time this examination was going on, they even opened his mouth to see if he had a tongue.

At length, Maquina gave the sign, and John spoke out, to the great surprise and delight of the spectators, addressing them in their own language.

They made a great burst of applause at this, saying that he was a man, like themselves, only he was white, and looked like a *seal*, alluding to his blue jacket and trowsers. They did not like this dress, and tried to persuade him to take it off, and put on one like their own.

The celebration here was similar, as far as John had had an opportunity of observing it, to the one held at Tashees.

During the visit, Maquina gave a particular detail of the manner in which he had obtained his prisoners, and related all that had happened concerning the ship and her crew, stating at the same time, the motives that had prompted him to the barbarous act.

The religious ceremonies were concluded by twenty men who entered the house, with arrows run through their sides and arms, having strings fastened to them, by which the spectators twitched, or pulled them back, as the men walked round the room, singing and boasting of their power to endure suffering.

Returning to Cooptee after this visit, the men in the canoe kept time to the stroke of the paddles, with their songs; and they reached home about midnight.

The time went off, employed in fishing, &c. at Cooptee, till the beginning of February, when an annual feast was to be given by Maquina, to which the whole of the Aitizzarts, and many of another tribe, were invited.

It was a scene of great gluttony, and so was almost the whole of the life at Cooptee; immense quantities of provisions being cooked, and destroyed with brutal lavishness.

On the 25th of February, the tribe returned to Nootka, which, notwithstanding the melancholy scene it brought to mind, was a matter of rejoicing to the unhappy captives, as it gave them the hope of seeing some vessel that might come to their relief.

Not long after the return to this place, a story was told to Maquina, by the *Cayuquats*, of twenty ships that were on the coast, coming to destroy him and his people for what they had done with the Boston and her crew.

This threw him into great alarm, and thus the objects of the false Indians, who had fabricated the report, was obtained.

Though John assured him that there was not the least truth in it, he would not believe him, but kept a strict eye on him and Thompson, regarding them with great jealousy, and would not let them go out of his sight, for fear of their going somewhere, to meet their countrymen from the vessels, to inform against him.

Soon after this, a death took place in the family

of the king.   A son of his sister, about eleven years old, and who was considered as a Tyee, died in the night, after having languished a long time in a kind of consumption or decay.

As soon as the breath left his body, all the men and women in the house set up such a yelling and howling, as waked the prisoners, and obliged them to leave the house to escape the noise, which was kept up till morning.

A great fire was then kindled, and in it Maquina burnt ten fathoms of cloth, in honor of the dead child, with whom he afterwards buried ten fathoms more, eight of the Ife-maw shells, and two small trunks, containing Captain Salter's watch and his clothing.

It was the custom of these people, whenever a chief died, to bury with him some of their most valuable articles.

Tootoosh, the husband of Maquina's sister, and the father of the deceased boy, had been one of the chief actors in the dreadful tragedy on board the

Boston; he had killed two of the men with his own hand.

This man, Tootoosh, had, a short time previous to the removal to Tashees, been suddenly attacked, while in perfect health, by a violent fit of insanity, during which he raved continually about the men, Hall and Wood, whom he had killed, and said their ghosts were by him all the time, to torment him.

He would swallow no food except what he was forced by his friends, to take into his mouth; and whenever he attempted to take any into his hand, he would withdraw it, saying he should be glad to eat, but the dead men would not let him.

No instance of insanity had occurred among these people within the memory of their oldest man; and the only way in which they could account for this was, by a superstitious belief, that the ghosts of the murdered men had been called back by the prisoners, to torment the murderer.

Maquina, when first made acquainted, by his sister, with the strange symptoms of her husband, took John and Thompson with him to the house, and, pointing at each, asked Tootoosh if they tormented him. He said, 'No—John good—Thompson good—Hall and Wood *peshak*,' (bad.)

Maquina placed food before him; but he said Hall and Wood would not let him eat, and continued in this state till a short time after the death of his son, when, after the most dreadful ravings, he grew exhausted and died.

Maquina became convinced that John and Thompson had no agency in causing the delirium, and the prisoners found that it was viewed by the natives, as a punishment sent by Quahootze, for the murder of the men, and to this they thought they owed their lives; as in several instances, when councils had been held, respecting putting them to death, the natives would not consent to it, and many of them talked about Tootoosh, in a way that showed they feared being visited themselves; and the king said he was glad his hands did not dip in the blood of the white men.

The madness of Tootoosh was terrible; he

would rave, kick, bite and spit at all who came near him, but the prisoners; but he would pat John on the shoulder, and call him good; and none could manage him but Thompson and he, who were, on this account, set over him as attendants.

It was a question with them, whether the insanity was occasioned by the death of a daughter, about fifteen years old, not long before, or sent immediately from the hand of God to make the natives tremble at their own crimes, and fear to do any thing against their lives, lest their punishment should be of the like kind.

CHAPTER XIX.

*Maquina goes a whaling—bringing in the whale—death and
burial service of the crazy chief—the king's jester—a mutiny
feared—a conspiracy—Thompson kills an Indian.*

Soon after the death of the boy, whose mother
had been obliged to bring him to Maquina's house,
to avoid the violence of his crazy father, the king
commenced his whaling excursions; but with so
little success that he returned day after day out of
humor, and once with a broken harpoon, and
nothing to pay for it, or for his toil.

John went to work and made him a good steel
one, which pleased him highly, and the first time
that he went out with it, he struck, with a death-
thrust, a noble whale; upon which, a signal was
given, and all the canoes were out to help tow
him in.

While the poor dying whale was dragged ashore,

the women were on the roofs of the houses, drumming with great violence, and mingling their shouts of exultation with the cry of, ' *Woocash! woocash, Tyee!*' and the men in the canoes were singing a song of triumph, to a slow tune, as the victim was brought to the land.

When he was cut up to be boiled, John had a handsome present of blubber, for making so successful a harpoon.

It should have been remarked that, previous to one of these whaling excursions, the king had a habit of going alone to the mountains, to pass a day or two in prayer for success in his business; and when he returned, wearing the red fillet and the spruce branch on his head, in token of humiliation, his manner was serious and gloomy.

Tootoosh died early in June, and his death occasioned another scene of mad sorrow, that was louder than his own crazy ravings had been.

The wailing and yelling was kept up, for about three hours; then the corpse was brought out of the house, and laid on a board before it.   A red fil-

MAQUINA'S RETURN FROM WHALING.

let was bound round the head, and a mantle of sea-
otter skin wrapped about the form.

It was then put into a box or coffin, with several
strings of the Ife-maw about the neck, and all the
most valuable articles possessed by the departed
chief, were laid into the coffin. Among these, were
several fine otter skins.

At night, the time of their burials, ropes were
passed round the coffin, and poles run through
them, by which the coffin was taken up, and borne
by eight men, followed by the widow and family,
with their heads shaved as a sign of mourning, to
the place of interment.

The grave was a small cavern in the side of a
hill. Here they deposited the coffin, and closing
up the cavern securely, returned to the house.

The next ceremony was performed by building
a large fire, and burning every thing owned by the
deceased, that had not been buried with him.
These were blankets, pieces of cloth, &c.

They were laid one by one, on the fire, by a
person appointed by the king, to the office who

was dressed out in his finest gear, with his. head
bestrewed with down, and who, as each article
was laid on the fire, would pour on oil to increase
the flame, and while it was burning, make a
speech, or show off some feat of buffoonery, to the
bystanders.

The funeral solemnities, if so we may call them,
were finished by Sat-sat, who performed one of
his best dances on the occasion, in honor of his
dead uncle.

The name of the man who had officiated as
priest in making the sacrifice, was *Kinneclimmets.*
He stood with Maquina in the relation of king's jester, on account of his tricks of mimicry and other
monkey traits, that raised him high in his majesty's
estimation.

He not only performed the part of buffoon, but
he had also the office of master of ceremonies at all
the feasts, and that of public orator. He harangued
the people, showed all to their places, and amused
them mightily with his antic gestures, his low wit,
and savage merriment.

In short, they seemed to think that all their enjoyment of a public occasion depended on the pranks of this speaking ape. Such a character was attached to the train of each tribe among the natives, and the title he bore was that of *Climmer-Nabbee*, which must have been a very comprehensive word, since it meant so much, enbodied in one great personage.

One feat that this man undertook, for the amusement of the company, on some feast day, was to eat to excess.

He first drank three pints of oil, and then engaged to eat four dried salmon, and five quarts of herring roe, mixed in a gallon of train-oil. But he failed in this; for, before he got through with his meal, the salmon proved that they were not quite so securely imprisoned in his stomach as they had been in the waves, and that they *could* 'get out' by the same mouth by which they had entered.

On one merry-making occasion, when a chief had brought home his new wife, the jester undertook to entertain the revellers, by passing three times through a large fire; but, happening not to be made of *asbestos*, he got so severely burnt, as to come very near dying for his folly.

Maquina was always delighted with any of this man's extraordinary performances, and sure to reward him with some present.

The frenzy and death of Tootoosh caused great alarm among the natives, lest a similar fate should await them; for John told the king it was, no doubt, a punishment sent by Quahootze, for the murder of the men.

This intimation, while they believed it, only soured them towards the prisoners, and when the king was out of sight, they would insult them, by calling them miserable slaves, asking them where their Tyee was; when they would answer by their own gestures, showing that his head was cut off, and that theirs should be also.

But they took good care, at these times, to keep out of the reach of Thompson's hand, the weight of which they had sometimes severely felt.

As the summer advanced, there was a great

scarcity of fish in their waters, and they were reduced to a state of great want, so as to be obliged to go sometimes without food, except what they got by gleaning for muscles and cockles among the rocks.

The natives not only showed, on this account, great ill-humor towards the prisoners, whom they suspected of using some conjuration, or some influence with Quahootze, but with true savage inconsistency, they reproached their king with having driven away the fish, by mingling the waters with the blood of the murdered white men.

But Maquina was usually kind to the captives, and always gave them a part of the best he had to eat. Sometimes he would make them presents, and when he feared a mutiny from his people, he would assure them that if a vessel came within a hundred miles of the village, he would let them send letters for their countrymen to come to their relief, and take them home.

Once he so far feared a general revolt from his people, that he would suffer none but John and

Thompson to keep guard over his person, night and day, and they had to go armed for the purpose.

He had, at this time, discovered a conspiracy between three of his chiefs, one of whom was his brother, against his life; and he suspected them to be linked in the plot, to another neighboring tribe. He, at this time, not only kept his white body-guard close to him on all occasions, but he made his men fire the cannon every morning, to let the other tribe know what they would have to meet if they came upon him.

In these hours of intimacy with the king, and of his dependence on them, John and Thompson complained of the insults and unkind treatment they had of late received from the natives.

Maquina told them, that it should not be so, and that they must let him know if ever any thing of the kind was shown them by any of the Nootkans; but if any of the strangers among them offered to abuse them, he said they might punish the offender by immediate death; telling them, at the same time, that they must take care always to go well armed.

The mutinous spirit of the people gradually subsided; but it was not long before Thompson availed himself of the liberty the king had given him.

He was at the pond washing clothes for himself and John, and a blanket for Maquina. Several of the Wickanninish came by, and seeing him, began to insult him, and to trouble him about his work. He warned them to desist; but not heeding him, one Indian, more bold than the rest, stepped on the blanket that was spread on the grass to dry, and trampled it under his feet.

Upon this, Thompson drew his cutlass and severed the Indian's head from his body. The others, affrighted at the deed, took to their heels and went off in a moment. Thompson then gathered up the blanket, with the marks of the Indian's feet and the stains of his blood on it, and the head wrapped in it, and carried it to the king, telling him the whole story.

He commended Thompson's chivalry, and gave

THOMPSON KILLING AN INDIAN.

him a present in token of his approbation; and the
other natives, learning what it was in the power of
the white slave to do, treated him and his companion with more respect and deference ever afterwards.

This deed of Thompson's was a terrible one,
and it is sad to think that necessity compelled him
to take the life of a fellow-creature. But it was an
act of self-defence, as much as any warfare is:
for though his life did not, at that moment, seem
threatened, there was no telling to what a dreadful
death these barbarians might have brought him,
had he not made them fear him.

CHAPTER XX.

*John is ordered to make arms—the king declares his intention
to go to war—expedition to Aycharts—attack and slaughter
of the inhabitants—return to Tashees—John is told he must
marry—going to select a wife—making choice of one.*

SOME time in July, Maquina told John that he
must set about making daggers for the men, Cheetoolths for the chiefs, and a weapon for him that
should strike the enemy on the head, while asleep,
and kill him at a blow, for he was going to war,
he said, with the *Aycharts*, a tribe about fifty miles
to the south, who had quarrelled with him during
the last summer.

John must have felt very badly on receiving
these commands, and knowing for what immediate
purpose his work was designed. He was, however,
obliged to obey orders, and following Maquina's
directions, he made his weapon in a different manner from any of the others

It was a kind of dagger, or spike, with a long iron handle, with a crook at the end where the steel spike went in, and at the other, a large knob, to resemble a man's head, for the eyes of which, he fastened in a couple of black beads, with sealing-wax.

The bend in the handle was to keep it from being wrenched away; and the weapon, being altogether a formidable one, and highly polished, pleased the king mightily. He would not allow any of the chiefs to have one like it, reserving its use exclusively for his own royal hand.

When all preparations were made, the natives manned about forty canoes, well armed with their dreadful instruments of destruction, among which were a few bows and arrows.

The bows, about four feet long, were drawn by a string of whale sinew; the arrows, of a yard in length, were pointed with copper, shell, or bone.

The expedition, of which John and Thompson were obliged to make two, set off in the night, to come upon and slay their sleeping foes.

They sailed during the silence of the night, and intent upon their dreadful purpose, about thirty miles up a broad river, the banks of which were covered with deep forests, till they came opposite the village they were about to depopulate; here they landed, and remained in perfect stillness till the moment of attack.

The town of Aycharts was situated on a hill, which being of difficult access, was a kind of fortress. The houses were about sixteen in number.

Maquina said he should not make the attack till towards the dawn of morning, that being the hour when the Indians slept the soundest.

At length, the awful moment arrived. The Indians left their canoes, and, crawling on their hands and knees, up a winding pass, they entered the dwellings of their slumbering enemies, while John and Thompson were stationed without, to stop such as might try to escape.

Maquina seized the head of the chief, and as he struck the death blow, he gave a terrible war-whoop, the signal for all hands to 'fall to, and spare not.'

A few of the surprised Aycharts fled into the forests, and escaped death; the others were all slain, or taken prisoners, to become slaves to Maquina.

The hand of Thompson was not slack in this terrible work. He slew so many of the unarmed enemy, that the Nootkans gave him the name of *Checkeil-sunarhar*, a chief who in former years had been a great warrior among them.

But John was very glad it did not fall to his lot to shed the blood of any. He only took four captives, whom Maquina, as a peculiar favor, allowed him to call his slaves, and who were to work exclusively for him.

All the old and infirm Aycharts having been put to death, Maquina set fire to the town, and laid every thing waste; after which, he and his men took their captives, and returned to their canoes to set sail for home, with their trophies of victory.

They were received at .the- village with great applause from the women, who drummed on the

houses, sang and shouted at their bravery and con-
quest; and Sat-sat performed one of his graceful
jump-dances in honor of their valor.

Soon after this, Maquina was strongly importuned to dispose of John. The Wickanninish king
sent his messenger, who, in their usual, formal
way, sat rigged for the occasion, in the canoe,
with his head powdered with down, and making a
display of the offerings his monarch would give for
the white slave whom he wanted to make arms for
him.

He had sent four slaves, two fine canoes, a large
quantity of metamelth and other things of great
value, as the price he was willing to give. But
Maquina rejected these splendid offers; for he prized John higher than all of them.

Towards the close of the summer, *Velatilla*, chief
of the Klaizzarts, came on a visit to Nootka; and
he also urged the king to sell John to him.

This chief was a fine-look ng Indian, of a complexion almost as light as that of a European. He
was well formed, very neat about his person, and

seldom wore paint, except on the place where, according to the custom of his tribe, the eyebrows had been plucked out.

His aspect was mild, and his manners pleasant; he usually had a smile on his face, and could speak English a little. He took great interest in John, and loved to converse with him in each of their languages; asking questions about his country, his friends and their modes of living.

He said that if he could prevail on Maquina to sell him, he would procure a passage for him to return home on board the first vessel he should discover on the coast.

This promise, John afterwards had reason to believe, would have been fulfilled, could Velatilla have prevailed on Maquina to part with him. For it was to this man's fidelity in delivering a letter in person to the master of a vessel, that the captives ultimately owed their deliverance; and this letter was the only one of sixteen which John wrote, that ever was delivered.

When he left Nootka, John made him a present

of a highly-polished cheetoolth, which he received with much pleasure and many signs of gratitude, and a promise to deliver the letter at the first vessel.

In September, the tribe returned to Tashees, and went over again the same business and mode of living that has been already described. But shortly after this removal, John was thunderstruck, if I may so speak, by a piece of information that was announced to him.

Maquina told him that a council having been held, it was agreed that he must marry one of the Indian girls; stating as a reason, that, as there were no vessels coming to Nootka, he would, no doubt, have to pass the rest of his life with them, and the sooner he conformed to their customs, and had a family of his own, the more happy and contented he would be.

This was giving poor John something more difficult than train-oil to swallow. He remonstrated vehemently against the step; but all to no purpose—he must either marry or die.

The only way in which the terms were softened,

vas his having the liberty to choose his squaw among the fair daughters of another tribe, if none of those of Nootka pleased his fancy, for a help-mate.

John cast his eye round, while his heart revolted at the sight of all the candidates for his hand, among the Nootkans; and he told the king he must look farther for a wife.

Accordingly, Maquina took about fifty men, in two canoes, with John, and a large quantity of cloth, sea-otter skins, and other articles, to purchase a bride, and set sail for Aitizzarts.

They reached this place about sunset, while John felt more like a victim going to the altar for sacrifice, than like a bridegroom approaching Hymen's altar.

Their sudden arrival at this hour, and without any known purpose, caused great alarm at the village. The men seized their weapons, and pre-paring for war, rushed violently down to the land-ing-place, making signs of defence, and threatening destruction on the supposed assailants.

But when the Nootkans had seated themselves quietly in their canoes, remaining perfectly still for half an hour, the villagers discovered their mistake; and the king sent his messenger to bid them welcome, and to show them to his presence.

Meantime, Kinneclimmets, the jester, priest, &c had made himself ready for the duties of the office he was to perform, by dressing and powdering with down.

The visitors, with their king at their head, form ed a procession, and moved with great order to the house of the Aitizzart monarch.

After being seated with due ceremony, and partaking of a sumptuous spawny and oily feast, Maquina told John to look round and see if he could find a girl that he liked.

His choice fell on one about seventeen years old, who sat beside her mother, and was the daughter of Upquesta, the king.

CHAPTER XXI.

Marriage ceremony—return to Tashees—John goes to house-keeping—is told he must change his dress—religious obser-vance—revenge of a husband towards his wife—removal to Cooptee—taking wild geese—return to Nootka—John is sick —a slave dies.

WHEN John had pointed out his future companion, Maquina made a sign to his men, who rose and taking the bridegroom by the hand, led him forth into the middle of the room.

Two of them were then despatched to the canoes to bring the articles with which the girl was to be purchased.

When the boxes were brought in, the men took out the articles, one holding up a musket, another a parcel of skins, a third a bundle of cloth, &c. while the jester, (or priest for the time) stepped up to Upquesta, telling him that all these belonged to John, and that he had come to offer them for his daughter whom he wished to have for a wife.

As he said this, the men threw the articles at the king's feet, with the stern air and look common for their expression of respect.

As they did this, the men and women of the village, who were all assembled to witness the ceremony, set up a loud cry of, '*Klack-ko—Klack-ko, Tyee*' (thank you, thank you, chief.)

Maquina then addressed the king, setting forth the good qualities of John, saying that he was as good a man as themselves; that he had only the fault of being white, which was more than over-balanced by his wonderful skill in making daggers, cheetoolths and harpoons.

He said he had so good a temper, that men, women and children at Nootka loved him; and that he would stay with them as long as he lived.

When Maquina began to make this eloquent harangue, which lasted half an hour, Kinneclimmets began to skip about the room, and continued performing all manner of pranks, till the speech was done.

Upquesta then took up the thread of discourse.

He set forth the amiable qualities of his daughter *Eutochee-exqua*, her accomplishments, and the love he bore her, as his only one.

He said, she was too dear for him to think of parting with her. But after talking some time in this strain, he finally consented to the union, saying that he hoped they would treat his daughter kindly, and that she would have a good husband.

As his speech finished with his consent, the jester began to call out in his loudest tones of voice, ' *Wacash*,' and spun round the room on his heels, like a top.

After this, Upquesta told his men to take the presents that had been laid at his feet, and carry them back to John; and to these he added a gift of two young slaves, to help his new son-in-law in fishing.

The company was then invited to a wedding supper at the house of one of the chiefs, during which the jester amused them with all sorts of monkey gestures and tricks.

The entertainment ended with a war song from

the men of each tribe, and a show of brandishing their weapons.

The company then returned to lodge at Upquesta's house; and in the morning, John received his bride at the hand of her father, with a charge to treat her kindly, which he promised to do, as the girl took an affectionate leave of her parents, and accompanied him, with an air of satisfaction, on board the canoe.

In addition to his other offices, the priest held that of king's steersman, and while guiding the canoe homeward with the lady of the forest within it, he regulated the song of passage till they arrived at the village.

On landing, their success was attended with great bursts of joy, and Maquina held a feast, after the women had received the bride, and conducted her to a place in the king's house, where she was to be kept, according to the custom of their country, for the space of ten days in retirement, seeing none but the women,—not even her husband,—till this time had elapsed.

After the ten days had passed, John had an apartment appointed him between those of the king and his brother.

His bride appeared, in every way, of an amiable and yielding disposition; and she was more fair and comely than any female Indian he saw except Maquina's queen.

Her form was good; her manners were gentle and affectionate; her features finely made and regular; her eyes bright and soft; her teeth small and white, and her hair very long and fine.

With this princess for a bride, John's household consisted, beside himself, of Thompson and Sat-sat, whose attachment to him still remained so strong, that he prevailed on his father to let him live with him.

Thus John went to *keeping house*, but in quite a different way from what he expected, when he took his father's blessing and his money, and set out from Hull to begin the world for himself.

Soon after his marriage, Maquina gave him another shock, by telling him, that, as he had married one of their women, he had become one of them for life, and he must adopt not only their habits, but also their dress; a command that was laid both on him and Thompson.

But John plead Thompson off, by urging that he was an old man, and changing his close garments for the kutsack, would probably kill him.

For himself, he got leave to wear the dress he had on, till it was worn out, it being then nearly past use.

Sat-sat, who was a very handsome and pleasant boy, became a great pet with the new-married pair, and they took much pleasure in decking out his little red person with beads, shells, jewels and other finery, which was very gratifying to his parents, and increased his fondness for his white friend.

When the annual thanksgiving came round again, John, being now identified with the natives, was told that he and Thompson, instead of being sent into the woods, must stay and help them pray to Quahootze to be good to them.

The ceremonies began as they did the year before; after which the tribe all stripped themselves of their ornaments; and binding on the fillet of humiliation, they repaired to the king's house with looks of sadness and dejection, and began to sing mournful songs, while the king kept time to the melancholy tunes by beating on his drum, or hollow plank.

The celebration was concluded by a boy, who entered the room with six bayonets run through his flesh in different parts. By these he was lifted and carried round the apartment, without making any visible signs of pain.

When John asked the cause of this scene, Maquina told him that formerly a man used to be sacrificed to Quahootze at the close of one of these ceremonies; but that his father had abolished the practice, and adopted this in its stead.

A great feast followed this religious observance, in which mirth and gluttony took the place of fasting and self-abasement.

Shortly after this, *Yeulthlower*, the king's brother, sent word to his neighbor John, that he wanted him to come and file his teeth for him.

John, suspecting no harm, obeyed the summons, and performed the office; which being done, and the teeth well sharpened, Yealthlower told him that the operation was to enable him to bite off the nose of a new wife that he had lately bought, and who refused to obey him.

John tried to dissuade him from this barbarous act; but he said he should certainly do it, if his wife did not behave better, for if she was not a good wife to him, she should be nobody's wife.

Not many hours after, he did as he had threatened, and sent his wife back to her father, with the loss of her nose as a *souvenir* of the attachment of her sharp-toothed husband.

About the middle of December, the tribe went to Cooptee, and recommenced their business of spreading boughs and setting wares under the water to entrap their food.

In addition to their other provisions, they had a plenty of wild geese brought them here, by the Esquates.

To take these geese, the Indians wove a sort of

net of strong fibrous bark, and going out on the water in a very dark night, with their canoes stuck full of blazing torches, they waited till the fowls, (goose-like,) attracted by the glare, gathered round it so near as to have the net thrown over them, and be taken.

One would suppose that none but a goose would do such a foolish thing as this; yet many a simpleton is so dazzled by fair and bright appearances, as to rush into as sure destruction as followed these delusive lights.

In February, the Indians went back to Nootka; and in March, John was taken violently ill of the colic in consequence of not being properly clad; and while he remained sick, a slave of the king's, having died of the same complaint, was thrown out of the house, and after lying some time without care, he was at length taken up and thrown into the water, as any dead animal would have been, to be put out of the way.

CHAPTER XXII.

John continues sick—he is divorced from his wife—she goes to her father—John recovers—an eclipse of the moon—a vessel arrives—consultation about the captives—a letter written to be carried by Maquina to the vessel.

THE manner in which this poor slave's remains were treated, had but a saddening effect on John, who expected soon to share the same fate, as his disorder threatened his life; and he seemed so disheartened, and so disturbed at every effort of his wife, who, though she did what she could to relieve him, was but an awkward nurse, that Maquina suspected he was dissatisfied with her.

He therefore told John that if he did not like his wife, his command or word could divorce them, and that he might be unmarried and let his princess return to her tribe.

So John, glad of the offer of liberty, told the

young princess that, as he should probably die, she would not have so good care taken of her at Nootka as she would with her father, and advised her to return and put herself under his protection.

With this advice the young Mrs. Jewitt took an affectionate leave of her supposed dying husband, telling him she hoped he would soon be better, and, leaving her two slaves to attend upon him, departed, with a suitable escort, for her father's town.

Though John was heartily glad of being relieved from his marriage obligations, yet this amiable young creature had ever been so kind and affectionate towards him, that he could not help feeling some sadness on account of her departure; and had he not viewed her as an insuperable objection to his ever leaving the place, or had he felt the event of his escape a hopeless thing, he would not have been willing to have lost her society.

By degrees he recovered his health, but with a heart sinking in despondency, as no signs of a vessel appeared on the coast, and no way of release from bondage opened to his view.

He had written many duplicates of his letter, imploring any into whose hands they might fall, to come to the relief of two unfortunate Christian men, held in bondage among a savage people, and representing the state of the deplorable life they dragged out, far from home and from a civilized country.

These had been distributed among the various tribes on the coast, for delivery; but as no vessel appeared, he supposed they must have been deterred from coming to the coast by hearing of the destruction of the Boston, which was a very large and powerful ship.

One thing that occurred during the winter of which I have been giving an account, I have not mentioned. So I will go back and relate it.

On the 15th of January, 1805, John and his fellow prisoner were awakened suddenly, in the night by a great noise and commotion among the Indians, who were all up and out on the roofs of their houses, which they had stuck full of torches, each in a bright blaze, while they were drumming on pieces of plank, shouting and singing with all their might.

On John's asking the cause of this tumult, they told him that a great cod-fish had come upon the moon, and pointing up to her, told him to see how the fish was trying to swallow her; and that they were endeavoring to drive him away.

It was soon found that the great fish was only an eclipse of the moon; but what gave rise to this odd superstition, the prisoners were never able to ascertain.

From the time of John's recovery from his illness, his life and Thompson's were dragged out, much in the way that has been described, until the 19th of July, when they had a sudden and joyful surprise.

As John was busily at work, making daggers for the king, the sound of cannon from the water came in three successive peals, upon his ear; and the cry of '*strangers! strangers! white men!*' as sent from mouth to mouth, among the natives, as they rushed into the house, telling him that a vessel was coming into the harbor.

This was a trying moment for the captives. The joy they felt may be imagined, but on the suppression of every symptom of it, seemed to depend their whole hope of escape; for they knew that if they manifested a strong desire to get away, the jealousy of the king and chiefs, lest they should inform against them, would occasion them to have their lives taken at once.

They therefore affected great indifference at the news; and the natives, wondering at it, asked if they were not glad to see the vessel. They said they cared very little about it, and kept at work.

Maquina coming in, and seeing them still employed, asked John if he did not know a vessel had come. He answered, Yes; but that it was nothing to him.

'What, John,' said the king, 'you no want go board?' John pretended that he cared very little about it, as he had become so reconciled to

ARRIVAL OF THE SHIP AT NOOTKA SOUND.

his present mode of living, that he felt very well satisfied not to give it up for his former customs.

A council was now held respecting the best way of managing the affair, and of disposing of the captives.

Some of the natives were for having them put to death, and for making the strangers believe that another tribe had destroyed the Boston.

Some, more humane, were in favor of the latter deception; but they wanted to have John and Thompson sent back a few miles into the woods, and kept out of sight, till the vessel should depart.

Others, of better feelings still, were neither for killing nor hiding them, but wanted to have them liberated and sent home.

But Maquina was loth to lose them in any way, yet he had a strange desire to go on board the vessel, to trade, and asked John if he thought he could do it with safety.

His people remonstrated against this step, for knowing what they had been guilty of, they feared being punished with the loss of their king; and recurred to the cruel treatment they had received from the whites in the instances which Maquina had related to John.

But John told them that if they had lived as long among the whites as he had, they would find they had nothing to fear; and said he was sure they would not harm the king if they received a request from him to use Maquina kindly.

Maquina then said he would go to the vessel and trade, if John would write a letter and tell the captain good about him; a proposal to which John readily acceded, so far as writing the letter was concerned; but the nature of the contents he reserved for his own choice, and wrote as follows:

'To Capt. ——, of the brig ——.

'Sir—The bearer of this is the Indian king, Maquina, by whose orders the American ship Boston, of Boston, Mass. was captured, twenty-five of her crew, the officers included, were inhumanly murdered, and the only surviving two held as slaves among the tribe.

'We, these unfortunate men, are now waiting for your assistance in our deliverance, and hope you will keep this man confined, putting in your dead lights, and having a strict eye to him, so that he may not escape you. If you will do this, we shall, in a few hours, be able to obtain our release.

> 'JOHN R. JEWITT, *Armorer of the Boston,*
> *for himself and* JOHN THOMPSON, *Sail-*
> *maker of said ship.*'

Such was the letter of recommendation which the royal messenger had given into his hand to deliver; and this was the 'good' that was written about him.

Great as John's deception and his departure from the truth may seem, at this trying moment, none can say that circumstances did not fully justify him in taking these measures, as they were the only means of effecting the escape, which, not made, might leave him to a cruel death.

My readers may suppose that John ran a great risk in giving these directions; but he knew very well that though the natives might threaten him in the most frightful manner, they would not dare to hurt him or Thompson, while their king was confined and in the power of the whites; and that sooner than have him injured, they would give up five hundred slaves.

CHAPTER XXIII.

NEVER did John undergo such a scrutinizing look from any other mortal, as Maquina gave him, when he took the letter, and told him to place his finger on every word and tell him its true meaning.

He had to forge a definition for every syllable, and to make it out, that he had told the captain how kind the king had been to him; and asked him to use him well, and give him as much biscuit and molasses, and rum, as he wanted.

Since his marriage, John had painted his face, like the others, which helped him now to tell a lie, without fearing his own countenance would contradict his tongue. When he had got to the end of the letter, with a false interpretation for every sentence, Maquina placed his finger on his name, and giving a glance that searched him through, said, 'John, you no lie?'

'Why, Tyee, do you ask me this? have you ever known me to deceive you?' said John. 'No,' was the reply. 'Why then,' said John, 'should you suspect me now?' Maquina's keen black eye was all this time rivetted upon his face, and when he had done speaking, the king ordered his men to get out the canoe for him to go to the vessel.

His people entreated him not to go, and his wives fell on their knees at his feet, imploring him to stay on shore; but he turned from them, and saying, 'John no lie,' left the house, and stepping into the canoe, ordered it to be paddled to the vessel.

He delivered the letter, and was immediately taken and put in irons, after he had been lured into the cabin to eat biscuit and molasses, while the men on board were arming themselves and preparing the manacles.

DEPARTURE OF MAQUINA FOR THE VESSEL.

He was in great terror at this reception, but made no resistance, only asking the captain to let one of his men come to speak with him.

The captain granted this request, but told him he was his prisoner till he ordered two men, who, he knew, were on shore in captivity, to be released.

The inhabitants were all waiting on the beach for the return of the canoe. As they saw it coming without the king, they showed much concern; and when it neared the land, and they learnt what had happened, they began to yell, tear out their hair, and run about in a most wild and terrific manner.

They told John, they knew it was a plot of his; and brandishing their weapons over him, said that they would cut him into pieces as small as their thumb-nails; that they would roast him alive, and head downwards, over a slow fire; and many other ways did they tell in which he should atone for his deed, but without alarming him; for he threw open his bear-skin garment, telling them to strike; that he was but one among many, and they might easily kill him, if they wished to see their

king hung up on 'that pole,' which he called the
yard of the vessel, pointing to it.

These threats were from the common people,
and the men. But Maquina's wives came round
John, and kneeling before him, begged him not to
let the white people hurt him; while poor little Sat-
sat kept fast hold of his hand, and crying as if his
heart would break, as he plead for the life of his
father, saying, ' Don't let him be killed ! don't let
him be hurt !'

John pacified them all by assuring them there
was nothing to fear, if they would let him and
Thompson go free; for, that this was a thing of
the captain's own doing, as no doubt, he had heard
of their being kept in bondage, and come to release
them.

This, they believed, though they, at first, cried
out so violently, that John had spoke bad about
Maquina, in the letter; and they now came and
asked what they must do to get their king safe
back.

John told them, the best thing would be to let

Thompson be sent on board, with a request to the captain to treat the king well, till he could come out towards the vessel in a canoe; and then to let Maquina get into a boat and be brought out, where an exchange of prisoners should take place on the water.

They were willing to let Thompson go; but they, at first, wanted John to remain on land, till the men of the brig should bring Maquina, and take him back.

But John knew better than to trust his life to a plan like this. He felt it would not be worth much on shore among the natives, with their king safe back, after what had now taken place.

He therefore told them, that the captain, who knew how they had treated the crew of the Boston, would never consent to their king's coming till after both their prisoners were safe in the vessel, unless he got within reach, so that he could speak to him, and tell him to let the king come off.

So when Thompson had got safe away from the shore and the people he had so long and so heartily detested, John told them if they would now take him, and paddle him so near that he could hail the vessel, he would call to have Maquina sent out in the boat, from which he might step into the canoe, when he, giving up his seat in it, would take one in the boat and go to the vessel.

This they consented to; while Sat-sat hung round John, begging him, since he was going away himself to leave him, to see that his father was given safe back to him:

John promised to do this, and, after taking an affectionate leave of the weeping boy, he hastened to the canoe that waited for him.

He took his seat so as to face the Indians, who paddled, and who, as soon as they came within hail of the brig, dropped their oars, and waited for the call to be given.

At this, John took out his pistols, and told them to proceed, or he would shoot them both dead in a moment.

Unprepared for an act of this sort, the Indians were so frightened, that they almost fancied themselves shot already, and seizing their oars, they literally paddled for their lives, till they got to the side of the brig.

We can never describe John's emotions; but we may imagine how his heart leapt for joy within his bosom, as his feet leapt on board the vessel of a Christian people.

The vessel was the brig Lydia, of Boston, Captain Samuel Hill, commander, who had been on the coast near Klaizzart, and received the letter from the chief, Ulatilla.

This interesting young chief had been faithful to his promise made to John, to see his letter delivered, and had gone out some distance to sea in his canoe, to give the letter with his own hand, into that of the captain, who on receiving it, proceeded directly to Nootka to the relief of the prisoners.

The crew of the Lydia rushed to the side of the deck as John sprang on board, with such a crowd of feeling of various kinds, as almost choked his utterance, while he tried to thank them for

JEWETT COMPELLING THE INDIANS TO ROW TOWARDS THE
VESSEL.

their kindness, and their congratulation on his escape.

In this confused state of mind, and overwhelming flow of feeling, with his strange and savage aspect, he must have filled the beholders with astonishment. Indeed, Captain Hill afterwards told him that he never saw any human figure look so wild as he did when he came to the vessel.

He was dressed in bear-skin; his hair was long and drawn up on the top of his head, and surmounted by a branch of spruce; his face was painted in true Indian style.

When he went below to see Maquina, who did not know that he had any hand in his confinement, he found him looking sad and dejected.

But his face brightened as he beheld his friend John's; and John asked leave of the captain to knock off the irons of the captive king, assuring him, that as long as he was with Maquina, there was nothing to fear from him.

He then gave, in presence of Maquina, a full account of the misfortune of the Boston; and Captain Hill thought Maquina ought to be put to death. But John plead in his behalf.

He said that, notwithstanding all the cruelty that had been shown to the crew, Maquina had often spared his life, when the cry of the people was for his blood.

He told Captain Hill that he had not only saved his life, but been uniformly kind, giving him a share of the best he had; and that he could never give his consent to the death of a man who had done this.

Maquina, who understood the nature of the conversation, kept interrupting it by asking, 'What are they going to do with me? are they going to kill me?' &c.

'John,' said he, 'you know that, when you were alone among five hundred warriors, all your enemies, I saved your life, when they demanded it—I was your friend. Now will you not do the same by me?'

John told him he would, and that he had nothing to fear if he would remain quietly till his people could bring out the remaining spoil of the Boston, which ought to be restored to its right owners. But this could not be done till the next morning, it was now so near night.

CHAPTER XXIV.

The things belonging to the Boston brought out—Maquina takes his leave of John—death of a young Chief—return of the vessel to Nootka, from the northward—Maquina visits her with skins—voyage to China—John hears from home by an Englishman—comes to Boston—finds a letter from his mother—concluding remarks.

THE Indians in waiting for their king, were then told that as soon as they would bring out what belonged to the Boston, they should take him back; but a strict injunction was laid on them, not to approach the vessel during the night, if they did not wish to be fired upon.

It was John's lot to pass the night with the royal captive, who would not let him sleep, but kept rousing him to answer some question about what was to be done with him.

Early in the morning, John hailed the natives,

and told them it was the will of their king that they should bring out the things belonging to the owners of the Boston.

They accordingly went to work with great expedition. To remove the cannon and anchors, they lashed two of the largest canoes together, and covered them with planks, and thus, with their burden upon them, towed them out.

In about two hours, every thing belonging to the ship and her cargo, that remained with the natives, was brought out; and Maquina was told that he might go home.

His canoe had come for him, bringing, in addition to the other things, all the skins which he had in possession, about sixty in number, as a present to the captain for letting him return, and without hurting him.

Such was Maquina's rapture, on being told he might go, that he sprang up, and throwing off his mantle that consisted of four fine skins, he gave it to the captain in token of his gratitude.

Captain Hill gave him, in return, a hat and great

coat. with which he seemed much pleased; and told him that he should return to that part of the coast in November, and he wished him to save all his skins for him to purchase.

'John,' said Maquina, turning to him as his interpreter, 'you know I shall then be at Tashees. But make a *pow*, (fire a gun) and I will come down to meet you here.'

As he stood at the side of the brig, ready to step into the canoe, he shook John cordially by the hand, telling him, he hoped he would come to see him again in a big ship, and bring much plenty blankets, biscuit, molasses and rum for him and his son, who, he knew, loved him very much.

He added, that he should never take a letter of recommendation to any one again, nor trust himself on board a vessel, unless John were in it.

The tears trickled down his cheeks, as he bade John farewell, stepped into the canoe, and was paddled off.

There was much in the character of this Indian king, which, had it been moulded by civilization,

PARTING OF JEWETT AND MAQUINA.

and purified by Christianity, would have been noble and delightful, and John had received so much kindness and protection from him, when he had none besides to help him, by human agency, that he could not help feeling a sort of sadness at his final separation from him.

An accident that happened on board the brig, greatly damaged the joy of John at his liberation.

A young Nootkan chief, who had had no hand in killing the crew of the Boston, and who was a fine fellow, happened to be one to help bring the muskets to the brig. As they were delivered, Captain Hill sat in the cabin, and snapped several of their locks. The young chief was near; when one of the muskets going off, discharged the contents into his body. The gun was loaded with swan shot.

John, on hearing the report of the gun, ran to the cabin, and found the Indian weltering in his blood with the captain, greatly shocked at the accider trying to help him. John assured him it was not intentional, as the captain had no idea of the gun's being loaded.

He said he was well aware of that, and after having his wounds bound up, he was put into a canoe and carried on shore. It was afterwards found that he languished some days, and then died of his wounds. He had always shown an amiable disposition, and been a good friend to the captives.

The brig made her excursion northward, and returned to Nootka in November. Here they followed Maquina's directions, and made the '*pow*.'

In a few hours, a canoe was seen. After having landed the king, it came out to the brig, and John recognised in it, the voice of Kinneclimmets, who asked if John was on board, saying that he had some skins to sell them, if he was.

John went forward and invited him and the others on board. They accepted, and told the captain that Maquina had some fine skins; but that he was afraid to come to the vessel unless John would come after him. This John agreed to do, if they would remain at the vessel.

They consented, and he got into their canoe, and paddled ashore. On his landing, Maquina was overjoyed to meet him. But when he asked for his men, and was told why they did not come, 'Ah! John,' said he, 'I see you are afraid to trust me, yet. But you need not have feared, for I should not have hurt you, though I should have taken good care never to let you go on board a vessel again.'

He then took his chest of skins, and got into the canoe which John paddled to the brig. He sold his skins, and seeming pleased with his visit, took a second leave of John, asking how many moons there would be, before he would come back to see him and Sat-sat, who, he said, wanted very much to come down with him from Tashees to see him.

The Lydia was bound to China. After a good voyage, with pleasant weather, she arrived, in due time, at Canton. Here there was an English ship, whose mate, hearing of two captives that had been released from Nootka, came to inquire about them.

This young man happened to be the son of a merchant at Hull, and next-door neighbor to John's father. He had heard of the fate of the Boston, and, like the rest of John's friends, supposed him to be long since dead.

Their meeting I will not describe. I will only say that the young man, whose name was John Hill, furnished John with comfortable clothing, some money, and many other articles that might add to his comfort on his passage, and after his arrival in America.

John gave him a letter to his parents, which arrived safely and speedily; for, when the Lydia arrived at Boston, after a passage of a hundred and fourteen days from China, which she left in February, 1807, he found a letter in the post-office, in answer to it.

The letter was from his mother, informing him that all his friends at home were alive and well. What else it informed him of, report saith not.

Neither have we any particular accounts of Thompson, after he gained his freedom. But I presume, he applied himself to the sail-needle again; and that he always took good care to keep clear of the shores of Nootka.

Our hero, John R. Jewitt, of whom we are now about to take our leave, acknowledged much kindness received from the gentlemen who had owned the lost ship, during his stay in Boston, Massachusetts.

How long he remained there, we have never heard, nor where he bent his way from that place.

The last I ever heard of him, gave information of his being a resident in Middletown, Connecticut, in the year 1815.

Whether he ever went through a second marriage ceremony, or not, I am not able to say; neither can I tell the line of life which he followed after his emancipation from slavery.

But I presume that wherever his lot was cast, and whatever that lot might be, he always carried about with him a grateful heart.

However sincerely he might have regretted his own waywardness, in preferring to take his own course in the choice of a profession, to hearing to the advice of his good father, I think he could never again have distrusted the overruling hand of Providence, or despaired of its help in a trying hour.

Experience is a faithful school-master, though, often a severe one, in whose hand the rod is sometimes used, even when the pupil may feel penitent for his faults of will or of judgment.

A LIST OF WORDS IN THE NOOTKIAN LANGUAGE, THE MOST IN USE.

Check-up,	Man.	Toop-helth,	Cloth.
Klootz-mah,	Woman.	Cham-mass,	Fruit.
Nrowexa,	Father.	Cham-mass-ish,	Sweet or pleasant to the taste.
Ho-ma-hexa,	Mother	Moo:-sus,	Powder.
Tanassis,	Child.	Chee pukes,	Copper.
Katlahtik,	Brother.	Hah-welks,	Hungry.
Klont-chem-up,	Sister.	Nce-sim-mer-hise,	Enough.
Tanassis-check-up,	Son.	Chit-ta-yek,	Knife or dagger.
Tamssis-kloots-mah,	Daughter.	Kli-k-cr-yek,	Rings.
Tau-hnt-se-tee,	Head.	Quish-ar,	Smoke.
Kassee,	Eyes.	Mar-met-ta,	Goose or duck.
Hap-se-up,	Hair.	Pook-shit-tle,	To blow.
Naetsa,	Nose.	Een-a-qui-shit-tle,	To kindle a fire.
Parpee,	Ears.	Ar-teese,	To bathe.
Chee-chee,	Teeth.	Ma-mook-su-mah,	To go to fish.
Choop,	Tongue.	Ar-smontish-check-up,	A warrior.
Ko k-a-nik-sa,	Hands.	Cha-alt-see-klat-tur-wah,	Go off, or go away.
Klish-klia,	Feet.	Ma-kock,	To sell.
O-o-l-chh,	Sun or Moon.	Kah-ah-pah-chilt,	Give me something.
Tar-toose,	Stars.	Oo-nah,	How many.
Sie-yah,	Sky.	I-yah-ish,	Much.
Toop-elth,	Sea.	Koin-me-tak,	I understand.
Cha-hak,	Fresh water.	I-yee-ma-hak,	I do not understand.
Mectla,	Rain.	Em-me-chap,	To play.
Queece,	Snow.	Kle-whar,	To laugh.
Nort-chee,	Mountain or hill.	Mar-kam-mah-sish,	Do you want to buy.
Klat-tur-miss,	Earth.	Kah-ah-coh,	Bring it
Een-puk-see,	Fire or fuel.	Sah-wauk,	One.
Mook-see,	Rock.	Att-la,	Two.
Mnk ka-tee,	House.	Kat-sa,	Three.
Wik,	No.	Mooh,	Four.
He-ho,	Yes	Soo-chah,	Five.
K k-k-elth,	Slave.	Noo-poo,	Six.
Mah-hack,	Whale	At-tle-poo,	Seven.
Klack-e-miss,	Oil.	At-lah-quelth,	Eight.
Quarl-lak,	Sea-otter.	Saw-wank-quelth,	Nine.
Con-con-ho-sa,	Seal.	Hycn,	Ten.
M-oo-watch,	Bear.	Suk-aitz,	Twenty.
So-har,	Salmon.	Son-jewk,	One hundred.
Toosch-qua,	Cod.	Hyce-oak,	One thousand.
Pow-ee,	Halibut.		
Kloos-a-mit,	Herring.		
Chap-atz,	Canoe.		
Os-wha-pa,	Paddle.		
Chee-me-na,	A fish-hook.		
Chee-mea,	Fish-hooks.		
Sick-a-minny,	Iron.		

THE LATER LIFE OF JOHN R. JEWITT.*

The captivity of John R. Jewitt among the Indians of Nootka Sound may have been hardly more spectacular than a number of similar adventures in the eighteenth and early nineteenth centuries. Yet there are few tales of Indian captivities which enjoyed so extensive an audience, for by a combination of timely chance and Jewitt's own restless showmanship his story obtained widespread currency along the eastern seaboard of the United States upon his return to civilization.

The early 1800's was an era when the glamour of trade with the Northwest Coast was a motivating factor in commercial circles. Inquisitive explorers and traders were pushing overland toward the western sea, and Americans generally were turning from European associations toward opportunities on their own continent. Culturally, the time was ripe for recognition of things American, and native themes began to enrich the product of authors in the quickening nation. Into this new atmosphere Jewitt brought the story of his captivity, and it is not surprising that through continual advertisement during his personal wanderings, the man, his tale, and something of the customs and inhabitants on distant Vancouver Island became familiar to a great many persons far removed from the scene of action. It is therefore of interest to recall that two of the country's most prominent men of letters laboured to perpetuate the Jewitt tale,

* The author wishes to express his gratitude to the following: Mr. Norman L. Dodge, of Goodspeed's Book Shop, Boston, for copies of the Jewitt letters; Mr. Julian P. Boyd, until recently the librarian of The Historical Society of Pennsylvania, for permission to reproduce the play-bill; the Curator of the Rare Book Collection of the Library of Congress for information concerning copyrights; the Chief of the Division of Music of the Library of Congress, the Chief of the Music Division of the New York Public Library, and Miss Joanna C. Colcord for information about the songs; the late Mr. Frank C. Deering for the photograph of the sole known copy of the broadside song; and two great-grandchildren of Jewitt, Mrs. Elwood Street, of Richmond, Virginia, and Mr. Frank R. Jewitt, of Cleveland Heights, Ohio, who searched for family letters and kindly furnished the pen-and-ink portrait.

British Columbia Historical Quarterly, Vol. IV., No. 3.

and that he himself enjoyed a short theatrical career on the sophisticated stage of Philadelphia.

The outline of Jewitt's biography through the period of his captivity is well known and briefly recounted. He was born in 1783 in Boston, England, of humble parentage, but his black-smith father destined his boy for a life more exalted than his own. However, the boy's entreaties led his father to teach him his trade, and a second ambition of the lad was gratified when he was permitted to sail as armourer in the ship *Boston*, of Boston, Massachusetts, under command of Captain John Salter. The vessel left England in September, 1802, and arrived in Nootka Sound on March 12, 1803.

Ten days after the ship's arrival the Indian chief, Maquinna, avenged what he considered an insult of the captain by seizing the vessel and murdering the officers and crew. Only Jewitt and John Thompson, sail-maker and gunner, of Philadelphia, were spared. Thenceforward these two were the servants of the chief, fashioning his weapons and performing his menial chores under conditions which at times approached starvation and ex-haustion. Through the months of slavery Jewitt managed by deception to continue a journal, using berry-juices for ink. This journal he carried with him when the two white men were rescued by Captain Hill, of the brig *Lydia*, in July, 1805. The *Lydia* remained on the Coast another year, departing for China in August, 1806, and arriving there in December. She left China in February, 1807, and sailed into her home port of Boston, Massachusetts, 114 days later.

Before the year was out, Jewitt saw to it that the above facts and the details of the captivity were preserved for posterity by publishing *A Journal Kept at Nootka Sound by John R. Jewitt*,[1] purporting to be the exact account which he had kept with such pains during his slavery. Yet almost nothing is known of Jewitt's life for the next few years beyond the fact that on

---

(1) Extant copies of the *Journal* are rare. To remedy this situation, Goodspeed's Book Shop, Boston, Massachusetts, in 1931 issued a limited edition of *A Journal Kept at Nootka Sound by John R. Jewitt, One of the Survivors of the Crew of the Ship Boston During a Captivity Among the Indians from March, 1803, to July, 1805*. Reprinted from the Original Edition, Boston, 1807—With an Introduction and a Check List of Later Accounts of Jewitt's Captivity, by Norman L. Dodge.

Christmas Day, 1809, he married,[2] this time according to the customs of his own people. His first wife was an Indian girl whom he alleged he had been forced to wed during his captivity. Thenceforward he probably spent at least a portion of his time relating his adventures, and perhaps for a livelihood peddled copies of his *Journal* from town to town, as it is known he did with his later publications.[3]

About 1815, however, Jewitt attracted the attention of Richard Alsop, Hartford merchant, and one of the renowned group of American authors of the time known as the Connecticut Wits. He was recognized as perhaps the cleverest of the clan next to John Trumbull. Alsop was one of the few millionaires of his day, and his great means permitted him the leisure to indulge in wide reading and in the polemic literary efforts of the local Federalist party.[4] According to his nephew, Theodore Dwight, writing in 1860, Alsop " had a peculiar taste of adventures," and drew from Jewitt the details of his captivity among the Nootkans. Repeated interviews were necessary to obtain the story, Dwight later remembered, and his uncle encountered difficulties from Jewitt's " small capacity as a narrator," and felt the task would have been much easier had the story-teller been a Yankee. Dwight was present at his uncle's house on at least one occasion when Jewitt was there and heard him sing Indian songs learned on the Northwest Coast.[5]

Alsop is recognized as a literary amateur and an "incorrigible imitator of late eighteenth century English modes,"[6] and his adaptation of Jewitt's tale is no exception to this rule. For his model in this instance he chose Defoe's *Robinson Crusoe*.[7] That

---

(2) Jewitt was married in Boston, Massachusetts, to Hester Jones, who had migrated to America at the age of 17 with an older brother, Lewis Jones. Mr. Dodge obtained this information from Mr. Frank R. Jewitt in a letter of March 9, 1931.

(3) *Journal*, Goodspeed edition, introduction, pp. xvi.–xvii.

(4) Vernon Louis Parrington, *The Connecticut Wits*, New York, 1926, pp. xxvi., xxxii.; S. T. Williams and J. A. Pollard on Alsop in *Dictionary of American Biography*.

(5) *The Historical Magazine*, April, 1860, quoted in Goodspeed edition of the *Journal*, p. xx.

(6) Parrington, p. xxxii.

(7) Theodore Dwight in *The Historical Magazine, op. cit.*

he succeeded in following his pattern is evident from the comments of a Philadelphia reviewer who remarked:—[8]

Our Connecticut *Redacteur* has . . . made a book which, while it may communicate a good deal of entertainment and information to all classes of readers, is peculiarly fitted for the perusal of the young; it forms, in fact, a very appropriate companion to Robinson Crusoe. It is, to be sure, not so entertaining: that was an advantage not to be obtained without bold deviation from real facts; but it is written in the same unaffected, perspicuous, and pleasing style, and though the writer never indulges in reflections or general remarks, a serious air of piety and morality reigns through the whole.

The book which Alsop wrote is, of course, *A Narrative of The Adventures and Sufferings of John R. Jewitt . . . ,* the first edition of which was printed at Middletown, Connecticut, in the spring of 1815, by Loomis & Richards. The records of the Clerk of the Court for the District of Connecticut show that Jewitt made application for copyright of the *Narrative* on March 8, 1815.[9]

It is not generally known, however, that on the same day Jewitt staked his personal claim to another production. Henry W. Edwards, the Clerk, recorded:—

Be it Remembered: That on the eighth day of March in the thirty ninth year of the independence of the United States of America, John R. Jewitt of the said District hath deposited in this office, the title of a Print, the right whereof he claims as Proprietor, in the words following to wit

"The Poor Armourer Boy, A Song."

The song was printed as a broadside, on a long sheet of paper, with a cut at the top depicting "The Ship *Boston* taken by the Savages at Nootka Sound March 22^d—1803." The cut is identical with the frontispiece in the March, 1815, edition of the *Narrative,* and at the bottom of the page is the copyright notice and the name of the printing firm, Loomis & Richards. The song itself is ornately "boxed" and is preceded by the explanation, "Imitated from the *Poor Cabin Boy,* of Dibdin, and adapted to the case of John R. Jewitt, a native of Boston, in Great-Britain,

---

(8) *Analectic Magazine,* June, 1815, vol. 5, pp. 493–496. Philadelphia, "Published and Sold by Moses Thomas, No. 52 Chestnut-Street."

(9) The record of copyright was obtained through the courtesy of the Curator of the Rare Book Collection, The Library of Congress.

the only survivor of the crew of the ship *Boston*, of Boston in
New England, who with the captain and officers were cruelly
massacred by the savages on the North-West coast of America."
The song itself is as follows:—[10]

> NO thrush that e'er pip'd its sweet note from the thorn
>   Was so gladsome and lively as me,
> 'Till lur'd by false colours, in life's blooming morn
>   I tempted my fortune at sea.
> My father he wept as his blessing he gave,
>   When I left him " my time to employ "
> In climates remote on the rude ocean wave,
>   Being but a poor Armourer Boy.
>
> Whilst amidst each new scene these " maxims of old "
>   Upheld me when grief did oppress;
> That a fair reputation is better than gold,
>   And courage will conquer distress:
> " So contented I brav'd the rude storm, dry or wet,
>   Buoy'd up with hopes " light painted toy,
> In thinking that Fortune would certainly yet
>   Deign to smile on the Armourer Boy.
>
> With our ship, on return, with riches full fraught,
>   We hop'd soon for Boston to steer,
> My heart it with exstacy leap'd at the thought,
>   " My eyes dropp'd through pleasure a tear."
> " But, alas! adverse fate so hard " and untrue
>   " Did all these gay prospects destroy,"
> For burn'd was our ship and murder'd our crew,
>   And wounded the Armourer Boy.
>
> For a long time in pain and sickness I pin'd,
>   With no one to feel for my woe,
> No mother, my wounds, as she sooth'd me, to bind,
>   No sister her aid to bestow!
> By savages fierce for years held a slave,
>   Did affliction my poor heart annoy,
> Till Hope dropp'd her anchor at last on the grave
>   As the birth of the Armourer Boy.

---

(10) Mr. Dodge, editor of the Goodspeed edition of the *Journal*, described
the song and quoted a portion of the first stanza on pp. 90–91. Mr. Dodge
obtained his information from the late Mr. Frank C. Deering. As far as is
known, the Deering copy is unique; letter of Mr. R. W. G. Vail, American
Antiquarian Society, January 4, 1940.

> From slav'ry escap'd, I, joyful, once more
>   Hail'd a civiliz'd land, but alone
> And a stranger was I on a far-distant shore
>   From that which my childhood had known.
> " If such be life's fate, with emotion I cried,"
>   Of sorrow so great the alloy;
> " Heaven grant that sole blessing that ne'er is denied,"
>   To the friendless Poor Armourer Boy!

The authorship of Jewitt's song is unknown. As to the original from which it was imitated, investigation reveals little. The Englishmen, Charles Dibdin and his son Thomas, were prolific writers of sea songs of the parlour type, which were sung widely in the theatres of the period and had a great following among English-speaking people. Jewitt himself was no doubt familiar with them, and it may be that he mimicked in crude verse a well-known song, hoping to obtain a popularity reflected from the Dibdin name.[11] Jewitt, however, made no definite statement of his authorship upon the broadside itself, and the song seems too good to be the work of the unskilled adventurer. It is possible, moreover, that Alsop, with whom Jewitt had been recently conferring, was prevailed upon to dash off the ditty as a supplement to the *Narrative* which he had just written. The verse hardly reaches the standard of Alsop's poetry, yet it differs in metre and rhyme from the style of Dibdin, and such alterations would require some ability with the tools of the trade. Furthermore, many phrases of the song are enclosed with quotation marks characteristic of the imitative tendency of Alsop.[12]

------

(11) Each Dibdin is credited with a song entitled *The Cabin Boy*, although neither caption contains the adjective " poor." Thomas's song bears the closer resemblance to Jewitt's, and concludes with the stanza:—

> My purse soon fill'd with Frenchmen's gold,
>   I hasten'd back with joy,
> When, wreck'd in sight of port, behold
>   The hapless Cabin Boy!

This song is found in *Songs, Naval and National, of the Late Charles Dibdin, with a Memoir and Addenda,* Collected and Arranged by Thomas Dibdin, London, 1841, p. 252. See also *The Songs of Charles Dibdin, Chronologically Arranged, with Notes, Historical, Biographical, and Critical* . . . , London, 1848, II., p. 385; *Dictionary of National Biography;* and Edward Bliss Reed, editor, *Songs from the British Drama,* New Haven, 1925, pp. 237–238.

(12) *Cf.,* Parrington, *op. cit.,* pp. 423–426.

Some substantiation for the claim that Alsop or some other person wrote the song likewise might be derived from Jewitt's use of the word " proprietor " rather than " author " in application for the copyright of the song as well as the *Narrative*.[13]

Jewitt's most important years in the purveyance of his tale seem to have been 1815 through 1817. It is not certain whether his publications of 1815, the *Narrative* and the song, were distributed through established book-dealers. It is recorded, however, that he himself set out in a wagon with copies of the book, to peddle them from town to town. Alsop is said to have regretted his part in the transaction, feeling that Jewitt thereafter " became unsettled in his habits by his wandering life in selling the book."[14] Just how far his journeyings took him is unknown, but he was seen dispensing his book from a one-horse wagon in Philadelphia. Another observer recalled seeing Jewitt with a wheelbarrow of books near the Capitol in Albany, the adventurer being readily identified by the large head-scar resulting from his wound during the capture of the ship at Nootka.[15] The few extant letters which Jewitt wrote to his family[16] indicate that he travelled at least as far north as Portland, Maine, as far south as Baltimore, Maryland, and even to Nantucket Island. It may be that from his stock he could offer two kinds of merchandise to suit the purses of his customers, the more expensive book and the cheaper broadside souvenir of *The Poor Armourer Boy*.

---

(13) It is perhaps presumptuous to suppose that the Clerk of the Court exercised a discriminating use of the terms in recording applications for copyright. Yet on the same day that Jewitt was twice listed as proprietor, another applicant appears as author. Furthermore, among the ten entries preceding and the ten following Jewitt's name, ranging in time between August, 1814, and September, 1815, there are recorded ten authors, one authoress, and nine proprietors. These facts were ascertained by Mr. David C. Mearns, of the Library of Congress, January 31, 1940.

(14) Theodore Dwight, *Historical Magazine, op. cit.*

(15) Inquiry concerning Jewitt in *Historical Magazine*, March, 1859, and reply in the same publication for April, both quoted in Goodspeed edition of the *Journal*, pp. xvii.–xviii.

(16) Jewitt's mother, Ann, writing from London in 1822, without knowledge of his death, requested two or three copies of the *Narrative*. She had heard of it, but could obtain no copies there. Copies of these letters, the originals of which are now in the possession of Jewitt's descendants, were kindly furnished by Mr. Dodge.

Regardless of the manner in which his productions were distributed, it is evident that Jewitt's *Narrative* attracted some attention. A reviewer in the *Analectic Magazine* of June, 1815, thought rather highly of the book, and took opportunity after the manner of the time to reflect upon the effect which atrocities against the savages by white captains had upon aborigines everywhere. Continuing he stated:—

We do not wish to give a disproportionate importance to this unassuming little volume, and shall therefore abstain from extract or analysis. It is proper, however, to state, that there is scarce any relation of savage manners which can lay higher claim to authenticity, than this simple narration. The facts are undoubted, and the book was prepared for the press by a literary gentleman of Connecticut, who has scrupulously abstained from all digression or embellishment of style, and restricted himself to a plain relation of the story in simple and correct language.

The form and size of the volume afford pretty strong proof that arts of literary manufacture are yet in their infancy among us. If by any chance these materials had fallen into the hands of one of the regularly-bred literary artisans of London, the lean narrative would have been larded and stuffed out with sonnets, sentiments, and philosophy, with digressions and disquisitions political, commercial, and economical, until at length, ' Jewitt's Voyages and Travels ' were fit to be ushered to the world in full pomp of quarto typography.

The reviewer then points out, no doubt with tongue in cheek, some of the comparisons which might be made between the native Nootkan hierarchy and British politics, and between the Indian ceremonials and songs and the English theatricals and literature of the time. As a whole, the *Analectic* writer seems pleased that simplicity rather than wordy elaboration pervaded Alsop's treatment of the tale.

The fact that the same magazine, in February, 1817, saw fit to review an 1816 edition of the *Narrative* further attests the book's popularity.[17]   This account begins with a straightforward summary of the volume. In his subsequent criticism, however, the author is less impressed with the quality of the book than was the first reviewer. He reports that since the magazine noted the first edition,

---

(17) *Analectic Magazine*, IX., pp. 141–165. The last sentence of the review states that Thompson died at " Havannah " not long after the *Lydia's* arrival, " and Jewitt is now distributing his Narrative through the United States."

it has been twice more put to press;—and it would at first sight appear somewhat singular that a book which is very badly written, and a great deal worse arranged, should have already circulated in the Northern States alone to the number (we are told) of about nine thousand copies. It is not recommended by those interior and exterior decorations which ordinarily get off a book of travels; for instead of an equilateral quarto, as " dick as all dis chees," accompanied by all manner of maps and plates and annotations,—we have here only a thin parallelogram of a duodecimo, " embellished " (the author thinks) with a single effort at an engraving, and blotted on the outside with two daubings, which are intended to represent the king of the Nootkians, first, in his visiting costume, and, secondly, in the act of harpooning a whale. All the interest of the volume is, therefore, derived solely from the nature of the facts which it contains. Of these we have already expressed our opinion; and have only to add, that although Jewitt has not been *had up* two or three times a day for a fortnight and crossexamined by the imposing Members of the Royal Society of London . . . , we know from the simplicity and good faith which appears in the narrative itself, and from the consistency which the author has preserved in telling ourselves the story at different times, that what he has given to the world is a faithful record of the facts.

In all, eighteen editions of the book have appeared in print. Two of these were issued in the British Isles. Of the two latest editions, one was published in 1896 by Clement Wilson, of London, with notes by Robert Brown, and the other is a German edition of 1928.[18] Peter Parley, astute editor and publisher for successive generations of young people, placed the story on the market in his series of Miscellanies under the title *The Captive of Nootka*, as a companion to such well-known works as the stories of La Pérouse and Alexander Selkirk.[19] This extensive and long record of publication is adequate testimony of the popularity of the *Narrative*.

---

(18) *See* Appendix B. This location list brings up to date the information in the Goodspeed edition of the *Journal* and the account of F. W. Howay in " An Early Account of the Loss of the *Boston* in 1803," *Washington Historical Quarterly*, XVII.. October, 1926, pp. 287–288, and the editorial note, *ibid.*, p. 311.

(19) *See* Appendix B. Earlier authorities, quoting Parley, whose true name was Samuel Griswold Goodrich, give the first publication date as 1832. Evert A. Duyckinck and George L. Duyckinck, *Cyclopedia of American Literature*, New York, 1855, II., pp. 311–313; and S. Austin Allibone, *A Critical Dictionary of English Literature and British and American Authors*, Philadelphia, 1872, I., p. 701.

The attention aroused by early editions of the *Narrative* no doubt accounts for the interest of the second great literary personage to be attracted by the inherent possibilities of the adventurer's tale. About the time Philadelphia intellectuals were reading the 1817 *Analectic* review, Jewitt was in conference concerning a new venture, the dramatization of his Nootkan experience, and in this undertaking it was his good fortune to enlist the services of James Nelson Barker.

Barker enjoyed a varied career. Not only was he a noted biographer and playwright but, in addition, he served as a soldier in the War of 1812 and held office in both the Philadelphia and Federal governments. Many of Barker's plays were performed in the theatres managed by William Burke Wood and William Warren in Washington, Alexandria, Baltimore, and Philadelphia. Historians of the theatre differ as to who took the initiative in proposing to Barker that he exploit the Jewitt theme. One authority contends that Wood and Warren " had the journalistic enterprise to commission Barker "; another investigator believes Jewitt took the lead.[20]

As early as March 10 advance notice was given of the Barker play in an advertisement of the Philadelphia Theatre: " In preparation, a Melo Drama, founded on the interesting narrative of Mr. John Jewitt, called the Armourer's Escape, or Three Years at Nootka, with new scenery, dresses, &c. &c. . . . ." Similar

---

(20) Actually, there seems to be no direct evidence as to which party took the initiative. Paul H. Musser, *James Nelson Barker*, 1784–1858, Philadelphia, 1929, especially pp. 72–74; Reese D. James, *Old Drury of Philadelphia; A History of the Philadelphia Stage, 1800–1835;* Including the Diary or Daily Account Book of William Burke Wood, Co-Manager with William Warren of the Chestnut Street Theatre, familiarly known as Old Drury, Philadelphia, 1932, p. 27.

Musser believes that the dispute with England over the settlement of the Oregon question provided a timely interest in any one who had visited that region under such exciting circumstances as Jewitt. There is no notice in the Philadelphia newspapers of early 1817 concerning the Oregon controversy, however, and Musser's contention seems to be unfounded. Perhaps he took his cue in this matter from his mentor and predecessor in the history of the theatre, Arthur Hobson Quinn, *A History of the American Drama from the Beginning to the Civil War*, New York, 1923, p.144.

announcements appeared in the newspapers in later editions.[21] On March 20 the advertisements became more detailed, stating that the new play would open the next evening, Friday, the 21st.[22] It was to be preceded by a tried and favourite comedy, *The Busy Body*, in accordance with the custom of billing two offerings an evening. The prices were the standard tariffs of the theatre, " Box, 1 dollar—Pit, 75 cents—Gallery, 50 cents." Doors were to be opened at 5.30 and the curtain was to " rise precisely at half after 6 o'clock." Notice was called to the play-bills for further details; but particular attention was directed to the concluding feature of the programme, the rendition of *The Song of the Armourer Boy*, to be sung by Mr. Jewitt himself. There were to be three performances—an unusual occurrence, inasmuch as a play was seldom repeated on successive evenings. On Saturday the accompanying piece was to be " the celebrated Play of Abaellino, The Great Bandit "; on Monday, the comedy *The Stranger*. Monday was also to be the occasion of Mr. Jewitt's benefit.

No copy of the play has been discovered, as the only manuscript was taken by Jewitt and has disappeared.[23] Description of the performance itself must then depend in part upon the advertisements already cited, but more upon the "bill,"[24] a broadside sheet delineating the play in such detail as to be, in the words of one author, a veritable scenario.[25] Therefore little comment upon the contents of the melodrama is necessary. It will be noted that efforts were made to sketch the narrative accurately,

---

(21) Philadelphia *Aurora*. Musser gives the 14th as the first date of preliminary notice; pp. 72–74. In addition to the *Aurora*, the following papers contained notices: *Political and Commercial Register*, *Poulsen's American Daily Advertiser*, *Democratic Press*, and *United States Gazette*.

(22) *E.g.*, the *Aurora*.

(23) Letter of J. N. Barker to William Dunlap, June 10, 1832, in William Dunlap, *A History of the American Theatre*, New York, 1832, pp. 379–380. Barker mistakenly recalled that the first performance took place March 24.

(24) *See* Appendix A for the text of the play-bill. The only known copy is in the collection of the Historical Society of Pennsylvania. The substance of the play-bill appears in Charles Durang, *History of the Philadelphia Stage, between the Years 1749 and 1855*, arranged and illustrated by Thompson Westcott, 1868, I., 1749–1818, p. 114. This consists of a series of scrapbooks in the library of the University of Pennsylvania.

(25) A. H. Quinn, *op. cit.*, p. 144.

even to the point of a faithful recording of the "costume, manners, ceremonies and superstitions of these extraordinary people," the savages of Nootka Sound.   To this end, Jewitt aided in directing the dancers, and, what is more important still, the adventurer was to take the part of the Armourer.   The other principal performers were regular members of the company's troupe, among whom were some of the most prominent actors and actresses of the period, including members of the famous Jefferson family.

It is interesting to speculate upon the manner in which the various and complicated scenes were staged.   In particular one wonders about the fourth and fifth scenes of Act I., showing the interior of Maquinna's house, and the Nootkan village during the eclipse of the moon, and the procession and ceremonials of the Indians in Act II.   How the audience was able to differentiate between the many tribes represented, and to what degree the showmanship of the day simplified for Philadelphia playgoers the elaborate "Ceremonies of the Bear" and the Nootkan War Dance, are questions open to conjecture.   That Jewitt held the centre of the stage as much as possible, and revelled in it, we can be reasonably sure.   While he had been actually among the savages the rigours of his captivity had been somewhat lightened by his cheery disposition and his willingness to recite and sing in his own tongue for the amusement of his captors.[26]   Now, on the stage, he entertained the more sophisticated Philadelphians in the language of the Nootkans, for near the end of the play he sang the Indian war song.[27]   The final curtain fell as Jewitt concluded singing his *Song of the Armourer Boy.*

What the audience in the Philadelphia or Chestnut Street Theatre thought of the play is not known.   William B. Wood, one of the managers, reported that "much curiosity and some interest were excited by so unique an exhibition."[28]   Some measure of the popularity of Jewitt's appearances may be derived from the

------

(26) *Journal,* Goodspeed edition, pp. xiii.–xiv.

(27) All editions of the *Narrative* contain the "War-song of the Nootka Tribe," with the instructions that it is to be "Repeated over and over with gestures and brandishing of weapons."

(28) William B. Wood, *Personal Recollections of the Stage; Embracing Notices of Actors, Authors, and Auditors, during a Period of Forty Years,* Philadelphia, 1855, p. 206.

record of receipts for the three evenings—$721.50, $339.75, and $301.50 respectively.[29] These comprise $1,362.75 out of the week's total of $2,202.75. The smallest sum was from Jewitt's benefit, and while the low receipts may partly reflect upon his performance it is well to note that the weather may have had considerable effect upon the size of the house. Manager Wood's diary records " fine " weather for the first night, " very mild " for the second, and " rain " for the final evening.[30] Even so, the average receipts for the three showings—$454.25—was considerably below that of the whole season, which was $596 a night.[31] Thus the play could not be considered an exceptional success, but neither could it be called a dismal failure, breaking precedent as it did by running three consecutive nights, and with the handicap of poor weather on one of these.

The brief theatrical career of John R. Jewitt had its beginning and its climax in *The Armourer's Escape* at the Philadelphia Theatre, but he was to have one more gala appearance before his curious public. There was, in the outskirts of Philadelphia, a summer amusement resort called Vauxhall Garden after its London model. Established in 1813 by John Scotti, Italian perfumer and hairdresser, the park or " circus " had enjoyed several successful seasons before opening again in the summer of 1817. The attractions were equestrian performances, fireworks, songs and speeches by famous celebrities, in addition to refreshments and relief in the cool of the suburbs from the heat of the city. Here we find Jewitt listed among Scotti's offerings. Nothing is recorded of his performance except the simple fact that he " sung songs dressed in Nootka costume."[32]

Later in the summer Jewitt was ill for eight weeks. " I have had," he wrote, " a complaint in my head attended with a fever which brought me verry low." But by October 12, when he

---

(29) R. D. James, *Old Drury*, p. 217. *Cf.* Wood, *Recollections*, p. 206.

(30) R. D. James, *Old Drury*, p. 217.

(31) *Ibid.*, pp. 27 and 217. By contrast with these receipts, one night in the previous week, because of snow, brought only $160. Further, the next performance following Jewitt's benefit was a benefit for the famous Jefferson, bringing $1,337.50!

(32) Durang, *op. cit.*, p. 115. *See also* Joseph Jackson, " Vauxhall Garden," in *Pennsylvania Magazine of History and Biography*, October, 1933, pp. 289–298.

signed the above letter to his wife, he had recovered his health sufficiently to journey to New York. Apparently the correspondence with Mrs. Jewitt had been enlivened by reference to his experiences with the drama. She had stated that she would rather learn he was a corpse than hear of his "being at the theatre," and he commented with feeling, "That is all nonsence and the State of Connecticut selfconceite, but no more of that I expect to heare enough about it. . . ."[33] Perhaps, before he was done with life, he did "heare enough about it," for Jewitt had essayed a venture on the stage in an era when many people considered a theatrical career far from respectable.

From this time forward, Jewitt's recorded life is less colourful. He probably continued his itinerant existence, sending back to his wife and children in Middletown occasional remittances and bountiful expressions of hope and pious wishes.[34] At long last he returned to Connecticut and permanent rest from his wanderings. He died at Hartford, January 7, 1821.[35]

If Jewitt was not widely mourned at the time of his death, at least his story kept his memory alive for succeeding generations. One of the two editions of his *Journal* and twelve of the eighteen various editions of the popular *Narrative* were published after 1821. Moreover, looking backward from the vantage point of great distance, we see Jewitt as one of the more picturesque characters of his day. Armourer, adventurer, author, peddler, and showman—these were the pursuits of his lifetime. To two men more skilled in letters than himself he provided inspiration for literary achievement of some merit and considerable interest. To countless persons along the eastern seaboard of the United States he brought knowledge of a far country, a land of savage

----

(33) This letter is cited in the Goodspeed edition of the *Journal*, p. xix. Mr. Dodge drew the natural conclusion that "at the theatre" meant "playgoer," but with the knowledge that Jewitt had experience on the bright side of the footlights it is possible to assume that this reference was to his acting.

(34) *E.g.*, Jewitt to his wife, from Boston, May 24, 1816. "I have enclosed to you fifteen dollars which I hope you will lay out to the best advantage you know Dear Hester what to do best and I am satisfied. I think it would be well to buy a few shad but you must do my dear as you think best. . . ." His letters are filled with solicitations for his children and sorrow at his failure to be as provident and accessible a parent as he should.

(35) *Journal*, Goodspeed edition, pp. xvii.–xviii.

make-believe. Jewitt's life and achievements thus served as links between the Northwest Coast and the awakening nation across the continent of America.

EDMOND S. MEANY, JR.

THE HILL SCHOOL,
        POTTSTOWN, PA.

APPENDIX B.

Location list of editions of Jewitt's *Journal* and *Narrative*.

The numbers assigned to the various editions in the following list are the same as those used in the check list on pages 87–91 of the Goodspeed edition of the *Journal*. The various abbreviations used are for the most part self-explanatory. *Journal* means an edition of *A Journal Kept at Nootka Sound by John R. Jewitt; Narrative*, an edition of *A Narrative of the Adventures and Sufferings of John R. Jewitt*, the original issue of which was adapted by Richard Alsop; *Captive*, an edition of *The Captive of Nootka*, the free adaptation of the *Narrative* compiled by " Peter Parley " (S. G. Goodrich).

It is believed that the three largest collections of Jewitt are in the library of His Honour Judge Howay, New Westminster, B.C.; in the Provincial Library, Victoria, B.C.; and in the Newberry Library, Chicago. These libraries are indicated in the location list by the symbols " H," " PL," and " N," respectively. It will be noted that Judge Howay possesses fifteen of the twenty items, the Provincial Library twelve, and the Newberry Library nine. Copies of three of the four editions lacking from all three collections have been located through the Union Catalogue of the Rare Book Collection of the Library of Congress. No copy of the 1837 edition of *The Captive of Nootka* has been found.

Of the twenty items listed, only the original 1807 edition of the *Journal* is believed to be very rare. The Goodspeed check list states that copies are in the possession of the American Antiquarian Society, the Boston Athenæum, the Boston Public Library, the British Museum, Harvard College Library, the Huntington Library, the Peabody Museum, the Provincial Library of British Columbia, and Mr. Frank C. Deering. To this list should now be added the name of Judge Howay.

1. *Journal*, Boston, 1807.	H. PL.
2. *Narrative*, Middletown, March, 1815.	H. PL. N.
3. *Narrative*, Middletown, July, 1815.	H. PL.
4. *Narrative*, New York [?1815].	H. PL. N.
5. *Narrative*, New York, 1816.	H.
6. *Narrative*, London, 1816.	H. PL. N.
7. *Narrative*, Wakefield, 1820.	H. PL. N.
8. *Narrative*, Edinburgh, 1824.	H. PL.
9. *Captive*, New York, 1835.	Boston Public Library.
10. *Captive*, Philadelphia, 1837.	No copy located.
11. *Narrative*, Ithaca, 1840.	New York Public Library.
12. *Captive*, Philadelphia, 1841.	H.
13. *Narrative*, Ithaca, 1849.	H. PL.
14. *Narrative*, Ithaca, 1851.	H. PL. N.
15. *Captive*, Philadelphia, 1854.	H. PL. N.
16. *Captive*, Philadelphia, 1861.	H.
17. *Captive*, Philadelphia, 1869.	N.
18. *Narrative*, London, 1896.	H. PL. N.
19. *Makwinnas gefangener* . . . [*Narrative*, in German], Leipzig, 1928.	Library of Congress.
20. *Journal*, Boston, 1931.	H. PL. N.

Some Notes

It is a good thing to give thanks....

Following in the footsteps of his illustrious father who did so much pioneer research and writing on the history of the Pacific Northwest, Dr. Edmund Meany, Jr., while an instructor in history at the Hill School, Pottstown, Pennsylvania, became interested in John R. Jewitt. Dr. Meany, a graduate of the University of Washington, received his doctorate from Harvard University in 1936. His article on the later life of John R. Jewitt was published in the *British Columbia Historical Quarterly,* volume IV, July 1940. Our grateful acknowledgement is made for permission to reprint the Meany research. What follows is a condensation of the July 1940 article.

The captivity of John R. Jewitt among the Indians of Nootka Sound may have been hardly more spectacular than a number of other similar adventures in the eighteenth and early nineteenth centuries. Yet there are few tales of Indian captivities which enjoyed so extensive an audience, for by a combination of timely chance and Jewitt's own restless showmanship his story obtained widespread currency among the eastern seaboard of the United States upon his return to civilization.

The early 1800's was an era when the glamour of trade with the Northwest Coast was a motivating factor in commercial circles. Inquisitive explorers and traders were pushing overland toward the western sea, and Americans generally were turning from European associations toward opportunities on their own continent. Culturally the time was ripe for recognition of things American, and native themes began to enrich the produce of authors in the quickening nation. Into this new atmosphere Jewitt brought the story of his captivity, and it is not surprising that through continual advertisement during his personal wanderings, the man, his tale, and something of the customs of the inhabitants of distant Vancouver Island became familiar to a great many persons far removed from the scene of action. It is therefore of interest to recall that two of the country's most prominent men of letters laboured to perpetuate the Jewitt tale and that he himself enjoyed a short theatrical career on the sophisticated stage of Philadelphia.

The outline of Jewitt's biography through the period of his captivity is well known and briefly recounted. He was born in 1783 in Boston, England, of humble parentage, but his blacksmith father destined his son for a life more exciting than life in England. The father wanted young Jewitt to be a scholar, so sent him to an academy in Donnington, England where he was exposed to Latin and mathematics, including navigation and surveying, but the son had a taste for the forge and workshop life followed by his father. With a taste for adventure young Jewitt in the summer of 1802 signed on with Captain John Salter, master of the ship Boston, to be an armourer (blacksmith) on a voyage to the Northwest Coast of America. They had on board a cargo of trade goods which they hoped to trade for furs, particularly sea otter. For this skilled work young Jewitt was to receive the salary of 30 dollars a month. There was a side agreement by which Jewitt had a right to purchase some furs for his own account, hoping that these could be profitably sold in China, which was then the market for such merchandise.

It was with high hopes that the Boston and its armourer sailed from England with a cargo consisting of "English cloths, Dutch blankets, looking glasses, beads, knives, razors," also a "great quantity of ammunition, cutlasses, pistols, three thousand muskets and fowling pieces." The ship sailed on the third day of September, 1802, in company with 24 American ships destined for New

England. For a few days the young armourer was seasick but when he became accustomed to the rolling motion of the ship a forge was set up on deck where he could ply his trade and a corner of the steerage was provided where he could work with a vise and tools in bad weather. He was employed repairing muskets and making "daggers, knives and small hatchets" for trade with the natives. At times he helped the sailors "taking in and making sail." The Boston sailed to Brazil, around the Horn and up the west coast of the Americas, arriving at Nootka Sound on March 12, 1803.

Ten days later the Nootka chief, Maquinna, avenged what he considered an insult from Captain Salter, by seizing the ship and murdering all the crew except John Jewitt, armourer, and a John Thompson, sailmaker, from Philadelphia. Through the 28 months of his captivity, Jewitt managed to keep a journal of his experiences using berry juices for ink. In July of 1805 Jewitt managed by some duplicity, to be rescued by Captain Hill, master of the brig Lydia. The Lydia remained on the coast another year trading for furs, then in August 1806 she sailed for China, arriving there in December. She left China in February 1807, and sailed into her home port of Boston after a voyage of 114 days. That same year young Jewitt managed to have the details of his captivity preserved for posterity by publishing his *A Journal Kept at Nootka Sound by John R. Jewitt.* For the next two years little is known of his life other than the fact that on Christmas Day of 1809 he married one Hester Jones, who had emigrated to America at age 17, in company with an older brother, Lewis Jones. It is assumed that Jewitt had spent much of the time after arriving in New England wandering the countryside selling copies of his book.

As the original Jewitt journal is not the world's most thrilling reading, the author might have drifted into the obscurity that befalls many amateur authors — except for the circumstance that about 1815 or earlier Jewitt came to the attention of Richard Alsop, a Hartford merchant and author. Alsop was a man of considerable competence and was said to be one of the few millionaires of his day. Alsop drew from Jewitt more details of his captivity. Using a little additional information and drawing liberally on his imagination he rewrote and expanded Jewitt's adventures and had this published in 1815 by Loomis & Richards of Middleton, Connecticut as *A Narrative of the Adventures and Sufferings of John R. Jewitt....* While the original journal had made no great impact on American literature, Alsop's narrative went through many editions and is still in print today, the newest edition being that of the University of Washington Press in late 1987. Jewitt applied for copyright of the Narrative March 8, 1815, and on that same day applied for copyright for a song intitled, "The Poor Armourer Boy, A Song." While thousands of copies of the Jewitt narrative were printed, and today are sought after by collectors of Americana, only one copy is today known of Jewitt's song. If we judge by the prosaic English of the original journal written on the west coast of Vancouver Island, it seems improbable that Jewitt wrote the lyrical and sentimental song. The authorship of the song is unknown but what is known is that Jewitt applied for a copyright on the date given above. It is of course possible that Richard Alsop wrote the song. In his application for copyright Jewitt used the term "proprietor" rather than "author" for both the song and the narrative. We do not know today if regular book stores carried the Journal or the Narrative but we do know that Jewitt himself peddled copies from a small horse -drawn wagon from Baltimore, Maryland to Portland, Maine, as well as a number of other towns in New England. He made at least one trip to Nantucket Island. It is possible that Jewitt sold one page copies of his song as well as the more expensive narrative book.

Jewitt also had a brief theatrical career in Philadelphia when he appeared in person in a play, "The Armourer's Escape," in 1817, in which he seemed to have and a playing and singing role. Death came at Hartford, Connecticut on January 7, 1821. The following year his mother in England, with no knowledge of his death, wrote requesting two or three copies of the narrative.

Beginning in 1835 juvenile edition of the narrative was published with the title *The Captive of Nootka*. Succeeding editions were printed in 1837 (no copy located). 1841, 1854, 1861 and 1869. The late nineteenth century printing of the narrative was in London in 1896, termed the Brown edition . The narrative apparently remained unprinted for 71 years until the Ye Galleon edition of 1967, after which a few more printings popped up. Thanks to Richard Alsop's colorfully written version of Jewitt's adventures we see John Jewitt, only 20 at the time of his captivity, as multi-facited, armourer, adventurer, author, book peddler, singer, showman. His journal and narrative have kept this memory alive for 181 years, from 1807 to 1988.

The names of the crew of the ship Boston are as follow:

Mr. John Salter, of Boston, America, *Captain*.
Mr. B. Delouisa, of Boston, *Chief Mate*.
Mr. William Ingraham, of New York, *Second Mate*.
Edward Thompson, of Blyth in the North of England, *Boatswain*.
Adam Siddle, of Hull, Yorkshire, *Carpenter*.
Philip Brown, of Cambridge, near Boston, *Joiner*.
John Dorthy, of Scituate, near Boston, *Blacksmith*.
Abraham Waters, of Philadelphia, *Steward*.
Francis Duffield, of Penton, England, *Tailor*.
John Willson, (Black) of Virginia, *Cook*.
William Calwell, of Boston.
Joseph Minor, of Newburyport.
Jupiter Senegal, (Black.)
Francis Martin, a Portuguese.
William Robinson, of Leigh, Scotland.
Andrew Kelly, of Air, do.
Thomas Willson, do. do.
Robert Burton, of Isle of Man, England.
James McClay, of Dublin, Ireland.
Thomas Plattin, of Blakeny, Norfolk, England.
Thomas Newton, of Hull, Yorkshire, England.
Charles Bates, St. James Deeping, Lincolnshire, England.
Peter Alstrom, Norway.
Samuel Wood, Glasgow, Scotland.
John Hall, Newcastle, England, *Seamen, all of whom were masssacred by the natives*.
John Thompson, of Philadelphia, *Sailmaker and Gunner*, and myself are the only persons of the crew who escaped this horrid butchery.

JOHN RODGERS JEWITT.

List of editions of John R. Jewitt

There are three versions of the Jewitt as follows:

A Journal Kept at Nootka Sound by John Jewitt	JOURNAL
Narrative of the Adventures and Sufferings of John R. Jewitt	NARRATIVE
Captive of Nootka, which seems to be a juvenile edition of the Narrative	CAPTIVE

H — *Howay*   PA — *Provincial Archives*   N — *Newberry Library*   GA — *Glen Adams Collection*

1. *JOURNAL*, Boston, 1807 — H PA
2. *NARRATIVE*, Middletown, March, 1815, Seth Richards, Ed. — H PA N GA
3. *NARRATIVE*, Middletown, July, 1815 — H PA GA
4. *NARRATIVE*, New York, 1815?, This is the undated Jewitt printed some time after 1815 and before 1834 and possibly printed at Ithica, N.Y. — H PA N GA
5. *NARRATIVE*, New York, 1816 — H GA
6. *NARRATIVE*, London, 1816 — H PA N
7. *NARRATIVE*, Wakefield, 1820 — H PA N
8. *NARRATIVE*, Edinburgh, 1824 — H PA
9. *CAPTIVE* New York — Boston Pub. Lib.
10. *CAPTIVE* Philadelphia, 1837 — No copy located
11. *NARRATIVE*, Ithaca, 1849 — H
12. *CAPTIVE* Philadelphia, 1841 — H PA N
13. *NARRATIVE*, Ithaca, 1849 — H PA
14. *NARRATIVE*, Ithaca, 1851 — H PA N GA
15. *CAPTIVE* Philadelphia, 1854 — H PA N GA
16. *CAPTIVE* Philadelphia, 1861 — H
17. *CAPTIVE* Philadelphia, 1869 — N
18. *NARRATIVE*, London, 1896 — H PA N
19. *Makwinnas gefanenger (NARRATIVE)*, Leipzig, 1928 — Library of Congress
20. *JOURNAL*, Boston, 1931 — H PA N
21. *Der Sklave der Nutka, Leben und Abenteur und Leiden bei den Indianern am Nutkasund*, Suttgart, 1954
22. *Narrative of the Adventures and Sufferings*, Fairfield, WA, Ye Galleon Press, 1967 — N PA N GA

23. *Adventures of John Jewitt Among the Indians*, London, n.d.
24. NARRATIVE, Toronto, McClelland and Stewart, 1974
25. NARRATIVE, Ramona, California, 1975
26. *Journal Kept at Nootka Sound* Garland Pub. taken from
    Newberry copy, 1976
27. NARRATIVE, University of Washington Press, annotated
    ed., 1979
28. JOURNAL, Ye Galleon Press, Fairfield, WA, 1988   N   GA

In addition to these known editions of John Jewitt we can add the 1948 fiction version of the NARRATIVE the Thomas M. Aumack *Rivers of Rain, Being a Fictional Accounting of the Adventures and Misadventures of John Rogers Jewitt, Captive of the Indians of Friendly Cove on Nootka Island in Northwest America*, Binforts & Mort, Portland Oregon.

I believe also that a condensed juvenile edition of John Jewitt was printed several years ago in eastern Canada, however I have not seen a copy of this and the Provincial Archives in Victoria has no knowledge of such an edition. Some bibliographies list an 1812 edition of the JOURNAL however, this is probably a ghost as I do not know of any existing copies of an 1812 edition.

SOME NOTES

Of the several hundred accounts of Indian captivities that have been printed, few were as widely publicized as the captivity of John Rodgers Jewitt by the Indians of Nootka Sound on the west coast of Vancouver Island. Instead of one account there were several, or to be more exact, there were three versions of Jewitt in book form, plus a stage presentation in March 1817, and a song "The Poor Armourer Boy," which Jewitt copyrighted March 8, 1815. This does not end the bewildering array of Jewitt material, for there was a twentieth century, drastically abbreviated edition of Jewitt written for children and printed in Canada, and in 1948 Binfords & Mort, a long established book publishing and commercial printing firm in Portland, Oregon, published the Thomas M. Aumack, *Rivers of Rain, being a Fictional Accounting of the Adventures and Misadventures of John Rogers Jewitt. Captive of the Indians at Friendly Cove on Nootka Island in Northwest America.*

Despite the circumstance that there are more than 20 different editions of Jewitt in one form or another and unquestionably thousand of copies were printed and sold, copies of Jewitt are not plentiful, any of the older editions are prized as top flight collectors' items, and many a man unable to locate a real Jewitt had picked up the Aumack fiction version. We can give a brief description of the three most important Jewitts:

1. A JOURNAL KEPT AT NOOTKA SOUND. This was the original work of Jewitt and is fairly dull reading. It has been printed only twice before this Ye Galleon Press editon, in Boston in 1807 and again in Boston by Goodspeed in 1931. Of the Goodspeed edition only 100 copies were printed and as many years have now gone by. The Goodspeed copies are frustratingly hard to come by. They do turn up now and then and have not sold for high prices but this is still a prized item and any collector who has one may well be proud of both its scarcity and its tasteful execution.

2. A NARRATIVE OF THE ADVENTURES AND SUFFERINGS OF JOHN R. JEWITT; ONLY SURVIVOR OF THE CREW OF THE SHIP BOSTON, ect. This was written by Richard Alsop after personal interviews with Jewitt. Thousands of copies of the Alsop version were printed in twelve different editions. These are highly valued by collectors of Americana but it is difficult to find a copy in anything like fine condition. Most copies

were read to pieces and surviving examples are likely to be in sorry condition with covers battered and the text pages exhibiting the usual signs of heavy use. The last English language printing of the Narrative was in London in 1896. This 1896 London printing is called the Brown edition and while collectors will by no means refuse it, copies are less desirable than the earlier printings. The 1896 copies are fairly common and persistent searching will usually turn one up. It should be mentioned also that there was a German edition of the Narrative, *MAKWINNA GEFANGENER*, printed in Leipzig in 1928. Despite its recent date this edition is most difficult to find on the antiquarian market. While not particularly valuable, when found this edition of Jewitt should be classed as a rare book. Such important rare book libraries as the Newberry in Chicago, the Provincial Archives in Victoria, B.C., and the library of the University of British Columbia, all rich in Jewitt material, do not have the Liepzig edition. Scholars who are interested may examine the Library of Congress copy.

3. CAPTIVE OF NOOTKA. This ia a rather free adaptation of the narrative as done by S.G. Goodrich and printed as part of the *Peter Parley* series. There were six editions of the Captive from 1835 to 1869, one of which, published in 1837, seems to have disappeared, at least to the extent that Howay and Meanie were unable to locate a surviving copy. It is presumed that several thousand copies of the Captive were printed in the six editions

of the Goodrich version, however any collector with one in his possession has an item of interest. The Goodrich version is perhaps slightly less desirable than the Alsop narrative but copies of the Captive often have the advantage over copies of the Narrative of being in better condition, particularly less foxing of the pages.

The above listing is of copies of Jewitt that exist. It is of passing interest that an 1812 printing of the Journal is listed in Sabin and some subsequent bibliographies. Apparently this is a ghost. It never was. This is a Jewitt that just isn't.

Fur trade on the Northwest Coast began in 1778 when Captain James Cook on his third and final voyage of exploration in the Pacific casually traded trinkets for sea otter skins, some of which were obtained in Nootka Sound. These skins were later sold in China and at such prices that the profit possibilities drew other men and other ships to that part of the North American Coast before the English and Spain had a strong claim as well, but the five thousand mile land journey across Siberia was a tremendous handicap to Russian trading and her ships were poorly constructed, although manned by men of great courage.

The raging flames of sixteenth century Spanish

exploration had long since burned to ashes and her rigid and impractical government structure with decisions coming from a great stone palace near Madrid, was hardly conducive to successful trading. Spain was still dreaming of wealth in terms of gold and silver swimming in clumsy galleons from the New World to the Old, but the truth was that she was fast losing her grip on this Brave New World and Spanish possessions in Latin America were soon in revolt against the mother country.

English vessels stepped into the breech and took over the immensely profitable maritime fur trade between the Northwest Coast and China. This was a golden opportunity but the Britishers fumbled the ball. They had ships on the coast when the weak but determined Colonies on the Atlantic Coast were fighting for their independence, and incidentally setting a pattern to be imitated by dissatisfied Spanish possessions. English trading vessels were required to be licensed by the East India Company or the South Sea Company, and while it was possible to have licenses with both companies this was expensive, so it was not usually done. In other words, one company governed the source of supply in the eastern Pacific Ocean, then called the South Sea; and the other company governed the market in the Orient. It was a long, cumbersome voyage to take furs back to England to be reshipped in different vessels for China. Ship captains from New England wanted none of this nonsense. They took trade goods directly to the Northwest Coast where they traded for fur which went directly to China. In Canton they purchased cargoes of silks and spices, valuable commodities in New York and Massachusetts. On land the well organized Hudson's Bay company proved formidable competition for U.S trading companies, but on the sea shrewd New England ship captains took the cream of the maritime fur trade.

The *Boston* was one more such U.S. vessel hoping to make an honest dollar on the day in March of 1803 when she hopefully anchored close in to shore and started trading for furs with the natives. All did not go well, in part because of mistreatment by the crew of a previous vessel. The natives rebelled and killed all the crew of the *Boston* except oneThompson, a sailmaker, and young Jewitt, the armourer, or to use a present-day term, blacksmith.

The vessel was accidentally burned and for the next 28 months Thompson and Jewitt were held captive by the Nootkan natives. Much of the time their life was hard and they worked at labor little above the level of Indian slaves. Thompson roundly disliked the natives and everything about the native way of life, while Jewitt, younger and with a more pleasing personality had some success in adjusting to primitive living conditions. His labor in fashioning weapons and trinkets was of value to the Nootkans and they rewarded him with a native wife. No such reward was given to the somewhat irascible Thompson and we are left with the impression that in Jewitt's case he was the somewhat reluctant recipient of girlish attention. It is of course possible that reticence in print in New England did not exactly correspond with life on Vancouver island in 1804, and in any event the friendship was not in all ways unsuccessful, for the Narrative says that Jewitt left this Indian princess with an infant son.

In the months spent as a captive Jewitt managed to keep a simple journal of his captivity, and also to send out a number of letters imploring release from his situation. One such message was delivered to Captain Hill of the *Lydia*, and by some duplicity Jewitt managed to get rescued and out of the hands of the Nootkan chief, Maquina. Despite the months of enforced labor and the massacre of the Boston's crew, it would seem that Jewitt found desirable qualities in Maquina and there was a considerable degree of respect and friendship between the two. It is probable that without the intervention and protection of Maquina, Jewitt and Thompson might well have shared the fate of the less fortunate members of the crew.

Nootka Sound has had a colorful history from the day in 1778 when James Cook anchored there. Ten years later in 1788 John Meares, captain of the *Felice* and William Douglas, captain of the *Iphigenia*, were there trading with the Nootkans. They stayed some weeks and built a small fort, also a forty-ton schooner, the *North West America*, the first sailing vessel ever built on the Northwest Coast. That same year two American captains came to Nootka, Kendrick in the *Columbia* and Robert Gray in the *Lady Washington*.

Next year all hell broke loose. Spain claimed the coast and belatedly sent Estevan Martinez and Gonzalo Haro to make a Spanish settlement at Nootka, and incidentally dispossession of the natives who obviously were there first. Ships of John Meares were trading illegally in the area, using Portuguese papers and sent them to Spanish authorities on the west coast of Mexico. Meares returned to England and screamed loudly at this insult to the British flag, although the ships had been trading in violation of English law. The French Revolution was in progress and Spain prudently avoided going to war with England over the Nootka incident. After some deliberation the Nootka Agreement was signed, by which Spain did not give up her title to the Northwest Coast but by which England acquired trading rights on the coast and the English vessels with Portuguese papers were released and returned.

England did not long dominate the maritime fur trade for by the 1790's United States' ships were dipping into the gravy and natives with furs to barter were showing a strong preference for New England knives and hatchets over the oriental trinkets so often offered by British captains.

After the rescue of Thompson and Jewitt the *Lydia* remained on the coast another year trading for furs. It might be mentioned that the Lewis and Clark expedition was at this time coming overland across the Rocky Mountains and through Lolo Pass and down the Kooshooskee (Clearwater), Snake and Columbia Rivers. This expedition arrived at the mouth of the Columbia early in November of 1805. The men spent a miserable winter at Fort Clatsop about seven miles south of the mouth of the Columbia remaining there until March 23, 1806, when they started back up the river on their return journey. The *Lydia* with Jewitt aboard made a visit ten miles up the Columbia in the spring of 1806 to take on a cargo of furs and must have narrowly missed meeting the Lewis and Clark party.

John Rodgers Jewitt was born May 21st, 1783 in Boston, Lincolnshire, England, the son of a blacksmith, Edward Jewitt. The father wanted his son to become a surgeon and when the lad was twelve he was sent to the academy at Donnington, about 20 miles from Boston. Life at Donnington appears to have been pleasant enough but young Jewitt preferred to work with the forge rather than with books. Eventually he was back with his father learning the trade of armourer or blacksmith. In 1798 the Jewitts, father and son and forges, moved to Hull, where the shipping of a busy port provided work for their trade. Four years later in 1802 the ship *Boston*,from Boston Massachusetts, arrived in Hull and the Jewitts did smith work for her. Acquaintance was made with Captain Salter, master of the *Boston*, and her mates. Delouisa and Ingraham. These men visited the Jewitt home with tall tales of far away ports and conversation about an impending voyage to Nootka Sound on the Northwest Coast of America. When the *Boston* finally sailed, on September 3, 1802, she carried with her young John Jewitt, to be armourer of the vessel. His pay was to be thirty dollars a month, a good wage for the day, and Edward Jewitt provided additional money to be invested in furs when they reached Vancouver Island.

The *Boston* crossed the Atlantic, touching on St. Catherine Island off Brazil, then keeping to sea until March of 1803 when she anchored near Friendly Cove, Nootka Sound, North America. Trading continued only a few days until tragedy overtook the ship and suddenly Thompson and Jewitt were the only men left of officers and crew.

The Jewitt captivity is described in some detail in the *Narrative of Adventures and Sufferings of Samuel Patterson* published in Palmer, Massachusetts in 1817. Patterson had sailed in the ship *Juno* under Captain John D'Wolf, which left Boston in the fall of 1804 and arrived off Vancouver Island early in April of 1805.

It would be good to be able to state here that Jewitt lived a long and useful life but the facts are otherwise. A diary kept by one of Jewitt's sons says that death occurred on January 7, 1821. The *Connecticut Courant*, a weekly paper, under the date of January 9, 1821, has this notice: "Died — in this city [Hartford], Mr. John R. Jewett [sic] aged about 37."

Jewitt had married Hester Jones, a girl of English birth, on December 25, 1809. In the eleven years and thirteen days of this marriage were born three sons and two daughters, and descendents of these Jewitt children are still living in Connecticut today. We have no information on the son of Jewitt born to an *Aitizzart* princess in 1805 but it is not impossible that some small amount of Jewitt blood remains in the Indians still living on the west coast of Vancouver Island.

WAR-SONG OF THE NOOTKA TRIBE.

*Commencing with a chorus repeated at the end of
each line.*

Hah-yee hah yar har, he yar hah.
Ie yie ee yah har—ee yie hah.
Ie yar-ee yar hah—ee yar hah.
Ie yar ee I yar yar hah—Ie yar ee yee yah!

I-ye ma hi-chill at-sish Kla-ha—Ha-ye-hah.
Que nok ar parts-arsh waw—Ie yie-yar.
Waw-hoo naks sar hasch—Yar-hah. I-yar hee I-yar.
Waw hoo naks ar hasch yak-queets sish ni-ose,
Waw har. Hie yee ah-hah.

Repeated over and over with gestures and brandishing of weapons.

NOTE.

Ie-yee ma hi-chill, signifies, Ye do not know. It appears to be a poetical mode of expression, the common
one for you do not know, being, *Wik-kum-atash;* from
this, it would seem that they have two languages, one
for their songs and another for common use. The
general meaning of this first song appears to be, Ye little know ye men of Klahar, what valiant warriors we
are. Poorly can our foes contend with us, when we
come with our daggers, &c.

The Nootkians have no songs of a historical nature,
nor do they appear to have any tradition respecting
their origin.

THE END.

Index

P

Q

R

S

The John Rodgers Jewitt captivity by Nootkan Indians on the west coast of Vancouver Island lasted from March, 1803 to July, 1805, when by some duplicity Jewitt escaped from the Nootka Chief Maquinna. There are three forms of the Jewitt captivity, the first being the *Journal*, written by Jewitt himself and published in 1807. This is a bit dull for reading and probably would have died in obscurity, the fate of many minor books, had not a competent and well to do man, Richard Alsop, interviewed Jewitt and re-wrote the account into a colorful and somewhat exaggerated version. The 1807 original is very rare, but was reprinted by Goodspeed's in Boston in 1931 in an edition of 100 copies, which of course sold out long ago. Ye Galleon Press printed the *Journal* in 1988 and this edition sold out as well. The Alsop edition entitled *A Narrative of the Adventures and Sufferings of John R. Jewitt; Only Survivor of the Crew of the Ship Boston, etc.* went through many editions and was reprinted by Ye Galleon Press in 1967. The third account of the John Jewitt captivity entitled *Captive of Nootka* is many times rarer than the Alsop 'Narrative' although it was printed six times from 1835 to 1869. It appears to be a revised and simplified version of the Alsop book and I know of no twentieth century printing of this edition. It is probable that there were a number of other instances of captivities of individuals that were never recorded. Some accounts that did see print are frustratingly rare, such as a party of Russians held captive on the north shore of Grays Harbor a bit past the year1800.

There are important collections of John Jewitt's adventures in the Provincial Archives of British Columbia in Victoria, B.C., and in the University of British Columbia in Vancouver, B.C., with the third leading collection probably held by the Newberry Library in Chicago.

This Ye Galleon edition of the Captive of Nootka was printed in the village of Fairfield, which is located in southeast Spokane County in Washington state, and one township removed from the Idaho line. Fairfield is on state highway 27 that runs between Opportunity and Tekoa. This edition was photographed from the original by Susan Paulson using a DS 660C 24 inch camera. The additional typesetting was by Teresa Ruggles using a Compugraphic 7300 Editwriter computer photosetter. Susan Paulson also stripped the film and made the printing plates. The sheets were printed by Garry Adams using a KOR Heidelberg press. Folding was also by Garry Adams using a Baum Dial-O-Matic folding machine. This was a fun project. We had no special difficulty with the work. This is the 579th title to come from Ye Galleon Press.

Sound
Broughton
Knight Ct.
ott Is.
C. Scott
Joseph B.
Beaver H.
Cove
Neville
Johnstone Str.
Quatsinnugh B.
Espinosa Inl.
Nachallos Ct.
Maquina B.
Port Brooks
Woody Pt.
Esperanza or Hope
Nootka I.
Guaquina Inl.
Friendly Cove
VANCOUVER ISL
Nootka Sd.
Estevan Pt.
Port St. Rafael
Flores I. C.
Clayoquot Sd.
Vargas I.
Bar